Eww.... You Homeschool?

HELP FOR SUCCESSFUL HOMESCHOOLING

Steffanie Williams

New Harbor Press
RAPID CITY, SD

Williams/New Harbor Press
1601 Mt. Rushmore Rd. Ste 3288
Rapid City, SD 57701
www.NewHarborPress.com

Ordering Information:
Quantity sales. Special discounts are available on quantity purchases by corporations, associations, and others. For details, contact the "Special Sales Department" at the address above.

Eww.... You Homeschool?/Steffanie Williams. —1st ed.

ISBN 978-1-63357-373-4

I want to thank my husband, for without his love and support I never would have homeschooled. David, you allowed me to follow my heart, and I am forever grateful. Thank you for reading the rough drafts of this book and giving me honest feedback that kept me focused and organized. Your honesty, wisdom and insight were as valuable in this project as they are in all aspects of our lives. I love you.

To my three precious daughters: Girls, you gave me some great material for this book and were wonderful companions on our homeschool journey. I love watching all of you live life so beautifully. Katie, thank you for being my social media extraordinaire, managing all of my social media. Emily, thank you for stepping in and helping with anything I need you to do. Mary Ruth, thank you for listening to me read the rough drafts of this book and for contributing your own chapter. You girls are shining examples of the benefits of homeschooling.

To my darling grandson: Noah, I thank God every day for you and the joy you bring to our family.

Thank you, Mom and Dad, for cheering me on always. Dad, I got my second wind! Also, to my Mother-in-law and Father-in-law, thank you for your love and support.

Thank you, Heavenly Father, for giving me this family and our story to share. Only with You is any of this possible. To God be the glory.

Contents

Introduction

"You must do the thing you think you cannot do." – Eleanor Roosevelt

66 "The supreme task of education is the cultivation of the human spirit: to teach the young to know what is good, to serve it above self, to reproduce it, and to recognize that in knowledge lies this responsibility." [1]

According to recent statistics approximately 2.5 million school age children from grades K– 12 are homeschooled. That is about 3.4% of U.S. students. This number will continue to rise. Here in my home state of Virginia we currently have 40,000+ homeschoolers. According to *Calvert Education*, the top 5 reasons that parents choose to homeschool their kids are:

1. Make a change from a negative school environment
2. Get a higher quality education
3. Improve social interactions
4. Support a learning disabled child
5. Educate children during a family relocation to another state or country

---

1. Hicks, David V., Norms and Nobility. New York: Praeger, 1981.

The website www.time4learning.com gives more reasons for a homeschool decision:

- Bullying
- A child's education needs not being met within the current school
- A desire to instill a specific worldview
- To provide the flexibility for a child to pursue his/her passion
- Concerns over school safety

Homeschooling is a popular choice today. As I write this introduction, our world has been turned upside down in the wake of COVID 19. More people than ever before are looking at homeschool as a viable option. A June 2020 ABC News poll found 45% of parents with school age children are not comfortable sending their children back to school in the midst of COVID 19. Educating children at home is becoming more and more popular. According to a *Real Clear* opinion poll taken on May 14, 2020, 15% of the 2,122 families surveyed are planning to homeschool their children this upcoming fall. If this statistic holds true for the remaining families who were not polled, this would mean 8.5 million children will be homeschooled in the fall of 2020. If you have been wondering whether you should try home education or not, this book will give you many reasons to homeschool as well as ideas, help, and encouragement as you embark upon your journey.

As you are considering your decision to homeschool, you may have some reasons why you think you should **not** try it. There are many different reasons why people think they cannot homeschool. Some of these are:

- I just don't have the patience for it.
- My kids won't listen to me.

- My kids and I argue about everything.
- I can't imagine being at home all day.
- I could never teach all of the subjects.
- I am not organized enough.
- I don't have a teaching degree.
- Maybe I could do it in elementary school, but there is no way I could teach high school classes.
- I am not creative enough.
- I want my kids to be social and have daily interaction with other kids.
- School wasn't so bad for me, it will be just fine for them.
- I will be with my kids all day, every day.
- It is too weird for me.
- I will have to work without a paycheck.
- I would have to give up my career.

Some of these may resonate with you. I had a few misgivings myself; I think it is completely normal to question what we are getting ourselves into, since homeschooling is a huge commitment. The starting point is to pray for direction and answers. It is always a good idea to put others' needs first. Selfless love goes a long way in overcoming obstacles. As homeschool parents we put our children's needs before our own. As you read about what I have learned, I hope you will glean the information you need to begin thinking of homeschool as a valid choice in the education of your children. And if you are someone who is already implementing homeschooling in your family, wherever you are in your journey, I hope this book will uplift and encourage you in your homeschool classroom. Hearing about someone else's ups and downs, failures and successes, is beneficial when traveling on a similar path.

In the early years of educating at home we would make our decision to continue to homeschool one year at a time. Each summer our family would have discussions about whether we wanted to continue to stay home for school. After the first few years, we no longer considered other options. Our questioning stopped, and we knew we were right where we were supposed to be. Homeschooling is without a doubt the best decision we ever made in the schooling of our children. Our girls agree that we have all been blessed by our commitment to homeschool.

CHAPTER 1

The Beginning

It is always insightful to look back over our lives and see how God has worked in our circumstances. Such is the case in the journey of writing this book. I originally began some fifteen years ago planning for it to be a how to book on the various aspects of parenting. Other than occasionally editing the content, the book has sat in a computer file for years. I learned to rest in the fact that one day God would show me His plan for it. I realized that I had to patiently wait to see what His plans were for the publication of this book. I did not start out anywhere near as patient as I am now, but time is a good teacher and has taught me that when it comes to this book and its outcome I needed to wait. I did wait, and after years of prayer and reflection I felt a leading to rewrite the content into a book that would tell of my family's journey in homeschooling. After a lot of prayer and a summer of writing, what you are reading are the fruits of the labor, putting on paper the many lessons I have learned in the years of schooling my children. We are approaching the last of our eighteen years of homeschool as our youngest is a high school senior. Eighteen years have come and gone too quickly, though there were times when I wondered if we would ever make it!

Remembering back to the beginning of our seeking and decision making processes about our daughters' educations gives me a sense of awe at what God has done. He was there through it all, even when I felt alone or confused. I remember the beginning all those years ago like it was yesterday. The questions were many, and the feelings of not knowing what to do were a real struggle. I battled with what was the right decision for my girls, what my husband would say, and what my family and friends would think. I remember having anxious thoughts that my decision could ruin both my children's social as well as their academic lives. That may sound silly to me now, but all those years ago I knew nothing about homeschooling. I was not sure if we could be happy living at home all day every day. I was not sure I wanted to give up my much loved career as an elementary school librarian. I did not know which path to take during that confusing time in my life. What I did know was that I wanted to do what was best for our girls. I was overwhelmed in many ways, and looking back I wish I would have had more trust in the Lord and the path He was clearing for me. This 54 year old would tell the 35 year old me to relax and trust God. He made a way for me, just as He always does. I think of one of my favorite poems and am thankful I traveled the different road, "Two roads diverged in a wood, and I took the one less traveled by, and that has made all the difference." – Robert Frost

In the pages of this book I will share with you:

- Why I decided to homeschool
- How I implemented our homeschool
- Schedules, goal setting and tips for discipline
- The importance of prayer, the influence of a godly parent, and the measure of success
- The beauty of time with your kids
- Ways to avoid too much busyness and achieve a balanced life

- A homeschool student's perspective (our youngest daughter shares her thoughts)
- Last minute musings

As you prepare, may reading these pages give you both direction and confidence. Expect to have difficult days but great days as well. Know that hard work pays off. Pros and cons are a reality in any aspect of life, and in our homeschool experience the pros have far outweighed the cons. You will find many blessings when you choose to put your family's needs above your own.

So, what caused me to begin questioning our family's education choices? Our daughters were in the public elementary school and we were happy there, but our oldest would soon be going to the nearby public middle school. The initial cause for our seeking out other options in education was that we were feeling unsettled about our child going to the public middle school. I was working in the public school system at the time, and I knew of incidents on the bus and in the school that made me anxious when thinking about her being part of that environment. I did not want her attending the middle school in the midst of the many issues and problems. In addition, I was seeing sweet kids that I taught during their elementary years all of the sudden acting like kids I hardly knew. The middle school years have always been an awkward time for many, but in today's world these years can be brutal. What is happening? I began questioning my long held belief that public school was the right and only choice. Understand that this was hard for me. I was a public school teacher surrounded by many public school teachers, who happened to be my family and friends. I had a public school mentality that I should leave education up to the experts. I now know that we parents are the experts when it comes to our own children, but this was a realization that took me a while to discover. I did not know any homeschool families until my girls danced at a local ballet studio with girls who were part of such a family. Through our time spent waiting on our daughters to finish dance class, this mom and I became good friends. To be honest, throughout the first year or so of our newly forged friendship I thought her choice to homeschool was just plain weird. She obviously was not leaving the education of her children up to the so-called experts. But as a result of our conversations, as well as witnessing her interactions with her girls, something was happening to my long held beliefs. I was impressed since this mama obviously had her act together! I began asking her questions and learning about what she was doing. I started pondering whether other teachers were truly the only experts when it came to educating my children. Maybe I could be the expert when it came to educating my kids, becoming a life-long learner alongside my children. Questions were arising in my mind that were never before there, and the time spent with this friend, as our girls were in ballet class together, laid the foundation for me to believe that homeschooling was a real option for our family.

Once I began feeling strongly that bringing my children home to school them was a definite possibility I needed to tell my husband what I was thinking. I was not sure how he would react, even though I talked with him many times about the conversations I was having with my homeschool friend about her school methodology. My growing excitement about everything I was learning was becoming evident to my husband. He and I had been discussing the possibility of putting our daughters in a local Christian school, because he too agreed he did not want our children going to the public middle school. The tuition payments at the private Christian school would have been a big expense, so we were on the fence about this idea. After months of talking about homeschooling, I realized I wanted to give it a try instead of sending the girls to the local Christian school. I realized that I could teach the same curriculum used at the Christian school and save a lot of money in not paying the yearly tuition. We were able to have a swimming pool installed with the money that we saved by not sending the girls to the private school. Looking back, I am thankful for that decision! We enjoyed our pool much more than we would have enjoyed going to the school!

My husband was supportive. Looking back I realize this was a big step for him. He thought the idea was radically different, but he trusted me. He knows when I am serious about something, and he knew I was serious about trying homeschooling. He had a lot of questions just as I did. But even with all of the questions, we had faith that God was leading us. It was one of the times in our life when we felt like pawns on a chess board; we were being moved around and just needed to let it, whatever it was, happen. We can trust that God will enable us, and the Holy Spirit will equip us to be the primary spiritual and academic teachers of our children. We had faith that He was in control and that He would lead and guide us. I began teaching our oldest daughter at home for the following school year, her 6th grade year. That first year we had one daughter at home and one still in the public elementary school. This did not work out. We needed to have everyone in one place, not juggling two different schedules. I thought at the time the right thing to do was to let our middle daughter finish elementary school with her friends, but she was resentful that we were all at home without her, that she was the only one with homework, and that she was not part of our daily activities. She was much happier once she was homeschooling with us. I praise God that He led our family on our homeschool journey. I thank Him for putting people in my life who helped and encouraged me. I praise Him for a supportive husband. I praise Him for this right decision for our family. I know that God, and God alone, has given me the background and experience to successfully write and share this book. He has worked in me through these many years and I can see clearly how all of my experiences have led me to this place. Here are a few of the realizations I have discovered through His Word, prayer, and through my life experiences:

- Rely on Me and listen to what I say to you from My Word.
- Take the leap of faith and school your children.
- I will enable you to continue on through the years.
- I blessed you with a degree in English and a background in teaching, specifically teaching high school grammar.
- I connected you with someone who needed an editor for his 100 short stories.
- I led you to a wonderfully supportive husband.
- I blessed you with three unique and lovely daughters to journey with you.
- I gave you the passion to share what you have learned with others who are thinking about traveling the same road.
- I gave you the experiences and insights that make up the pages of this book.
- I blessed you with a beautiful life story to share with others.

I realize God has prepared me for such a time as this.

CHAPTER 2

The Next Steps — Research and Reach Out

A fter making the decision to begin home education, my next step was to research. I am happy there are many more resources today than there were back in the early 2000's. With the current rising popularity of homeschooling there is naturally a demand for more resources. I read various books about homeschooling and sought advice from the people God was putting in my path. It was clear to see that once we made the decision to homeschool, God opened doors for me to meet more homeschool families. "Picking their brains" was beneficial for me. You may not know all of the questions to ask at the beginning, but talking to homeschool families gives you the opportunity to hear their stories. Talking about how they do what they do is a good place to start. These families are a wealth of information, and it is valuable to gain their perspectives.

It is important to reach out to home educator groups. These groups are available in most areas of your state. I have belonged to each county/city group wherever we have lived. We have resided in five different counties/cities in Virginia over the past

18 years, and each location has active home educator groups. You usually pay dues to be a part of these groups. Each group's website is helpful in giving valuable information such as area activities, organized fieldtrips, information on state homeschool laws, testing information, books and resources for sale, etc. States also have education associations. In our state we have the Home Educators Association of Virginia (HEAV). According to the HEAV website, their purpose is to:

- Help and encourage parents to fulfill their God – given rights and responsibilities to educate their own children
- Provide information and advice to homeschooling parents regarding home education and family life
- Support and protect the rights of parents to teach their children at home through legislative initiatives and contact with representatives in the Virginia General Assembly and United States Congress
- Educate the general public, educators and elected officials through personal contacts, the media, lectures, seminars, workshops, conventions, and newsletters concerning the benefits of home education and the Constitutional right of parents to educate their own children
- Provide information to home-educating parents, the general public, the media, and elected officials regarding the Virginia Code, pending legislation, and court cases as they relate to homeschooling
- Direct interested parents to local homeschool support groups for support and encouragement
- Assist homeschool support groups by providing information, resources, leadership workshops, and training seminars

Another Virginia homeschool group is The Organization of Virginia Homeschoolers (VA Homeschoolers). The group's website states, "Our goal is to provide homeschooling support to our members, as well as accurate information about homeschooling to Virginia's families, school divisions, legislators and policymakers, the media and the community at large."

Another group to look into is the Homeschool Legal Defense Association (HSLDA). This group is a trusted movement leader that makes homeschooling possible by caring for member families and protecting and securing the future of homeschooling. Though you may never encounter a legal issue related to your homeschooling, it is beneficial to look into the HSLDA and your own state homeschool group. State homeschool associations provide additional benefits such as information to help you get started, a list of support groups, newsletters designed to update you on current information, and educational and recreational events and activities happening in and around your state.

Your state homeschool group is a wealth of information about what you need to do to begin to legally homeschool in your state. In our state of Virginia, which is a moderately regulated state, we have three basic options for homeschooling:

1. The Virginia Home Instruction Statute (parents must meet specific educational criteria, file a Notice of Intent to Homeschool, comply with immunization requirements, and submit evidence of academic achievement annually)
2. The Certified Tutor Statute (for certified tutors/ programs)
3. The Religious Exemption Statute (for those with a sincere religious objection)

You will need to decide which option you will use in your homeschool. Next, you will need to file your notice of intent to homeschool with your local school division. You can call your local school board office, and they will send you the paperwork you will need to fill out and send back to them. It is your responsibility to send this information in to the school system each summer. In Virginia we have an August deadline. I always send the form our local school district requires, as well as the yearly test results (also a requirement in our state), as soon as our school year ends in May. Our state accepts several tests including the Stanford 9 and the California Achievement Test. We always test in the spring of the year. Note that in Virginia the PSAT and the SAT test results can be submitted for the year's testing requirement. This is good to know because I had planned to test with the California Achievement Test (just as I always do) in the spring of my daughter's sophomore year. She had already taken the PSAT earlier in the spring. Thankfully, I found out she did not have to take the CAT since the PSAT score took its place for the school system's requirement, and I was able to pass this information on to a mother who was also getting ready to double test her daughter. My daughter was happy to know that she was finished with spring homeschool testing once she started taking the PSAT and SAT tests. Once you have filed the required paperwork with your county/city school system, you can begin planning and preparing for your school year.

There are many approaches/methods to homeschooling. You will need to choose which method best suits your family. Here are several:

- Classical – In this approach there are 3 stages of learning, the grammar, dialectic, and rhetoric. This method relies heavily on reading the classics. Memorization is key in the elementary years. The student studies Latin in high school. Socratic Dialogue is also an important tool used in the later high school years. This method is excellent for teaching kids to be thinkers and to search out answers for themselves.

- Charlotte Mason – This approach is based on the teaching of 19th century Christian homeschooling pioneer Charlotte Mason. A key concept in this method is that the student has short periods of study coupled with lots of reading, nature observation, and memorization. Students have journals and portfolios instead of tests and quizzes. This approach incorporates the best books, fine arts programs, core academic lessons, and nature studies into a holistic and personalized program for each homeschooler.

- Eclectic – In this approach one uses a little bit of this and a little bit of that, pulling from a variety of curriculum. This approach incorporates lots of field trips.

- Unschooling – In this approach the students are in charge of what they want to learn. When something piques their interest, they dive deeper into learning about the subject. This method builds on natural gifts and talents.

- Traditional Homeschool – This approach uses a traditional curriculum such as Abeka or Bob Jones University Press. You teach each subject with a student textbook and a teacher's guide and you chart the student's progress with tests, quizzes, and grades.

- Unit Studies – This approach integrates all of the subjects into one study. For example, if you were studying Colonial America you would study the history, geography, science, and math that pertained to the period. I have known families who have had a lot of fun with this one, incorporating the art, music, food, games, etc. of the time period being studied.

- Waldorf Homeschooling – This approach is based on the ideas of Rudolf Steiner and emphasizes the importance of educating the whole child in body, mind, and spirit. Younger children learn with an emphasis on art, music and nature. Standard textbooks are not used. Older students are taught to reason for themselves. There is a lot of free time with this method. This approach recommends teaching curriculum, subjects/topics in blocks of 3 – 6 weeks of in – depth study. This keeps children focused on one subject at a time rather than switching gears multiple times a day. This method emphasizes the child's imagination and fantasy.

- Montessori – This approach emphasizes "errorless learning". A child learns at his own pace. Children are allowed as much unscheduled time as possible. This method believes children are drawn to what they need. Learning centers are set up in the home with themes pertaining to culture, music, art, etc. This method emphasizes real life experiences.

Here is further well consolidated information in the following list of options from www.workingathomeschool.com:

Traditional "School at Home" options –

- Abeka (one of our favorites)
- Alpha Omega's Switched on Schoolhouse
- Alpha Omega's Life Pacs (we used these for a few years in late elementary/early middle school science)
- Bob Jones University
- Rod & Staff
- Calvert School
- Christian Light

Charlotte Mason options:

- Ambleside Online
- Queen Homeschool Supplies
- Five in a Row
- Sonlight
- Winter Promise

Distance Learning Options:

- Bob Jones University Distance Learning
- Alpha Omega's Switched on Schoolhouse
- Calvert School
- K – 12
- Abeka Distance Learning (We tried this, but our daughter did not enjoy learning solely in a distance learning classroom.)
- Time4Learning
- Liberty Online Academy
- K 12 International

These distance learning programs are tuition based, and they absorb the responsibility of developing lesson plans, grading assignments, and providing homework support. There are also websites with extra learning resources such as Khan Academy. Khan Academy's website is easy to use and features more in depth and detailed lessons and learning resources in math by grade level, science, computing, arts, humanities, economics, and finance. There is also test prep for the PSAT, SAT, and MCAT. Our daughters utilized Khan Academy for PSAT and SAT test prep and found it valuable. CoreKnowledge.org, a nonprofit working for educational excellence, offers downloads of free resources for children pre K through 8th grade.

Unit Study Options:

- Weaver
- Konos
- Five in a Row
- Tapestry of Grace
- My Father's World
- Winter Promise

Classical Education Options:

- Classical Conversations (We have used this program for the past 6 years.)
- My Father's World
- Tapestry of Grace
- Veritas Press
- Memoria Press
- Learning Adventures

After researching various methods, I decided to start out with the Traditional "School at Home" option. This method fit our learning style and was not out of my comfort zone. Through the years, we have become a bit more eclectic with our approach and have tried snippets of other methods. As I gained more experience and confidence, I was able to try methods that were out of my comfort zone. It was fun to experiment and explore, and it helped keep our schooling interesting. For our youngest daughter, we switched to the Classical approach as she entered 7th grade. It is helpful to have an open mind and a bit of an adventurous spirit when it comes to experimenting with different methods. Sometimes the best approach may be a melding of several ideas tailored to your child's uniqueness.

Once you choose a method, you are ready to peruse curriculum. I like the company *Rainbow Resources* because they have a website with over 4000 homeschooling and educational products at discount prices. That is a lot of choices! The resources are listed together under the headings of science, math, history, electives, etc. This is an organized way to research the many companies that sell homeschool books. You can look at the many publishers who have science curriculums for example, and read descriptions of their products. Rainbow Resources' customer service does a great job answering curriculum questions. After quite a bit of research, I chose Abeka for all of our school subjects except math. Saxon was my math choice. Abeka and Saxon suited our traditional education style, wanting to use traditional textbooks, as well as quizzes and tests.

It takes a lot of time and patience to weed through all of the curriculum to choose what is best for your family. Realize this is normal and do not get overwhelmed or frustrated. I found that looking at one subject at a time helped me. I took a few days to read about various science curriculums until I found one that interested me. Next, I took time to research the math curriculums. I did the same for spelling, writing, history, etc. I wish someone would have told me to enjoy the process and to realize the blessing I had in the freedom of choosing what my kids would be learning. It is a blessing to be able to "paint your own canvas" as you choose resources.

Here is a list of some popular homeschool curriculum:

- Abeka
- Alpha Omega
- Apologia
- BJU Press (Bob Jones University)
- Christian Liberty Press
- I. E.W. (Institute for Excellence in Writing)
- Math – U – See
- Mystery of History
- Saxon Math
- Singapore Math
- Switched on Schoolhouse

- Wordly Wise

If accreditation is important to you, check first to see if the program/method you choose for your classroom is accredited. You can contact your own state's Department of Education for accreditation guidelines. My local public school system's website informs me, "For information regarding the Virginia Board of Education's Regulations Establishing Standards for Accrediting Public Schools in Virginia, also known as the SOA or Standards for Accreditation, refer to VDOE's Standards of Accreditation webpage. For additional information, please visit the VDOE Private Schools and Home Instruction web page at http://www.doe.virginia.gov/studentsparents/privatehomein-dex.shtml." If there is a chance you might send your child back to public school in the future, accreditation information is important to know. It is a good idea to check with the school to see what program of study they will accept to enroll your child back into the system in the proper grade level. I have known of instances where homeschool students are held back a year when they re-enroll in public school, because the school system would not accept the homeschool curriculum the family used. Checking with your area school's guidance counselor or the school system's website will give you this information.

Homeschool conventions and book sales at homeschool co-ops and other homeschool groups are great places to peruse curriculum and find good bargains. There is a used book sale in our area every summer. When you join your local home educators' group there is often a website where members are able to post books for sale. I have both bought and sold books in this way. Various homeschool publishers host curriculum fairs at homeschool conventions. They post on their website the locations and times where they will be, with their resources set up, so you can check it all out. For several years, I attended an Abeka book sale that was within an hour's drive of my house and was able to ask questions and see all of the material. There is something to be said about the ability to pick up a book and look through it, especially when you are not familiar with the publisher's offerings. Check to see if a company you are interested in will send out samples. Abeka is one such company and will send you samples of their curriculum. If you are interested in the Classical Conversations curriculum, they do not label grades as 7th, 8th, 9th, etc. Instead their grade levels are as follows:

- Challenge A – 7th grade
- Challenge B – 8th grade
- Challenge I – 9th grade
- Challenge II – 10th grade
- Challenge III – 11th grade
- Challenge IV – 12th grade

This program has 117,000 students located in all 50 states, the District of Columbia, Puerto Rico, and 15 foreign countries. Their website, *www.classicalconversations.com* will give you more information if you are interested. The Classical Conversations Curriculum has been a huge blessing to our classroom.

As you choose your curriculum a question to think about is, "What type of learner is my child?" When deciding which textbooks or academy to use, take into account what will help your child be the best learner. Is your child hands on? Does your child like to read? Does he need repetition to learn? Is he a visual or auditory learner?

An example of this decision making process is whether or not to use Saxon Math, which is not a math course for everyone. It is not a set of thirty of the same problems to work on to cement the new concept into memory. It keeps bringing in math concepts from previous lessons. A problem set in Saxon Math will have continual review of past concepts with just a few math problems from the day's lesson added to the mix. If your child needs a lot of math repetition on the new concept just learned, then this curriculum may not be for him. If you do want to try Saxon Math and you are not sure which year/level your child should use, you can find information on the website www.Sonlight.com under the heading Saxon Math Placement. There you will find an easy to follow guide since Saxon books are skill – level books, not grade – level books. This will help you decide which level your child should use.

Another example of your child's learning style driving your curriculum choice is if your child has trouble reading or does not enjoy reading, you may not want to start with the Classical approach. There is extensive reading in a classical education.

Again, reach out to homeschool communities/groups in your area. These groups give you opportunities to ask questions about methods, curriculum, and learning styles. In the early years, we joined a Co-op that met every Friday and an area homeschool activity day that met once a month. I was able to fellowship with the moms, while the girls had a blast with their newly formed friendships. These friendships followed them all the way through school and even beyond high school gradua-tion. Belonging to such groups helps you to feel connected and less isolated.

In our area Co-op that met every Friday from 9:00 – 3:00 my children were enrolled in five classes. This is where my oldest two girls took their high school sciences and labs. They were able to take physical education class as well. They were a part of elective classes such as drama and speech. This weekly Cooperative of talented and dedicated parents/teachers was a great opportunity for me to get the extra help I needed es-pecially with sciences and physical education. My girls loved Fridays and the opportunity to learn in fun classes alongside their friends.

Our family also participated in a Homeschool Activity Day that was sponsored by an area homeschool group. This took place at a local church on the 3rd Thursday afternoon of every month. There were many elective class choices such as cooking, magic tricks, drama, art, dance, etc. This was a fun opportunity for the girls and another time to hang out with their friends. These gifts of interaction helped us feel connected. We always came away from these group activities feeling refreshed. We enjoyed the break from one another, as well as the fellowship with others. Reach out and join whatever support groups are available to you. Sign up for various activities. Some ideas are: church youth group, swimming lessons, hiking club, chess team, local pet shelter volunteer, sports teams, music ensembles, theatre troupes, local homeschool groups and activities, and the list goes on. Get your kids out of the house to interact with others and to have various experiences. One of our oldest daughter's favorite activities was a monthly quilt club, where she made a quilted placemat. This is how her love of quilting began. One of our middle daughter's favorite activities was a monthly swimming club. She loved going to the area aquatic center with her friends. One of our youngest daughter's favorite activities was a monthly book club. She looked forward to getting together with her group and discussing the chosen book of the month.

I hope you have a reliable support system of family and friends. This support goes a long way in protecting us from failure. For me, it was looking to like-minded individuals who were already homeschooling because all of my family and friends were public school teachers or supporters. Homeschool was weird to them, and they were not as supportive of my ideas early on. They wondered, "What in the world are you doing?" If you are in the same boat, give family and friends, who initially do not seem very supportive, some time. It only takes a short while for most people to see the excellent results of homeschooling. My family and friends eventually came on board once they saw the results. One of my dearest friends, a public school teacher, as well as my Mother-in-law, also a public school teacher, became some of my biggest advocates, telling others about how wonderfully our homeschool works.

With the support of area homeschool co-ops and homeschool organizations, you will find information pertaining to book fairs, sports, field trips, dances, science fairs, book clubs, art and music classes, etc. in your area. This is how I found out about many wonderful opportunities that I never would have known about otherwise. My girls participated in craft days, quilt making, science experiments, dances, holiday parties, book clubs, swim lessons, as well as other activities because of excellent planning and execution by our area homeschool groups. If you are interested in your child participating in sports, there are many organized homeschool sports teams. These teams often compete against their area's Christian/ Private schools. Statewide law, individual districts, and schools make the decision regarding homeschool participation in public school sports. Ten states currently force public schools to allow homeschoolers access to sports. These states are: Arizona, Colorado, Florida, Idaho, Iowa, Maine, North Dakota, Oregon, Utah, and Washington. The national site for Homeschool Sports Network (HSPN), www.hspn.net, is a website listing all-season homeschool sports nationally, sorted by state. HSPN advertises that they are America's source for homeschool sports. The National Homeschool Football Association, www.homeschool-football.com, is a website listing information for the national homeschool football championship. This site lists homeschool football teams with their website links. In the state of Virginia alone, we have 39 homeschool athletic associations/groups listed on the HEAV, Home Educators of Virginia website. This is just a sample of what is available. Some of the sports represented are: football, basketball, volleyball, soccer, rugby, track/ cross country, cheerleading, wrestling, softball, baseball and tennis. There are also many homeschool swim teams. Research what your state and local area have to offer.

Reach out to your church family. Through the years, as we have visited various churches, I have witnessed firsthand that some are more homeschool friendly than others. Our family has been blessed to be part of congregations that, for the most part, have been supportive. These bodies of Christ followers can offer you help, support and accountability. Every homeschool group we have been involved with has been housed in a church building, our co-ops, activity days, Classical Conversations, etc. The staff of the churches where we meet are gracious and welcoming. Without being a part of a church fellowship, we would not have been plugged into many of our group activities. Being connected to our church family gives us a network of people who have access to resources. I found out about the girls' piano teacher, art lessons, swim lessons, etc. from church friends. Being active in your local church and doing life together with fellow Christians also gives you much needed encouragement and prayer support. It is a blessing to be with like- minded individuals who uplift you in your vision to homeschool in a way that glorifies God.

There is a wealth of information and encouragement available to you through a homeschool search on your media device. You will find many that offer homeschool ideas and support. There are also several online magazines that I have used through the years. Some of my favorites are:

- www.homeschoolingtoday.com – articles pertaining to parenting, special needs, literature, science, art and general and practical homeschool issues will be found on this site.
- www.theoldschoolhouse.com – articles that explore the benefits of home education, giving help and support since 2001.
- www.homeschoolingparent.com – articles that have tips, learning resources, free stuff, and curriculum

since 1999. I recently enjoyed the "Free Homeschool
Printables for July" – July 7, 2020.
- www.themailbox.com – this magazine has worksheets
and lessons for all grade levels. There are entire themed
units and printable activities. I especially like this one
for the holiday activities. I subscribed to this when the
girls were in the younger grades. It gave us fun games,
crafts, ideas and activities.

You will find there is an endless supply of info out there. The
biggest challenge is having the time to sift through the ideas to
find what best suits your style, personality and values.

The average cost of homeschooling ranges from $700.00
to $1,800 per year according to www.time4learning.com.
This price includes the cost of curriculum, school supplies,
field trips and extra- curricular activities. A year of Classical
Conversations in the Challenge level high school years is at
present (2020-2021) $1,375.00 plus the cost of the curriculum,
which is usually a couple hundred dollars.

As you research and reach out, I encourage you to be confident in the fact that you know your child better than anyone
else. Be confident that you can make the right decisions for
him. You can choose what is best for your family. Godly friends
and influences help in the years of schooling that can sometimes seem difficult and long. Pray for open doors to finding
homeschool friends and groups who will help you get through
your days in uplifting ways. Even though what we do is called
homeschool, it is important to be part of bigger communities.
This allows for opportunities, experiences and friendships that
both you and your child would miss if you stayed at home all of
the time.

CHAPTER 3

Many Reasons to Homeschool

We researched and reached out and found many reasons why homeschooling was for our family. Our initial reason for homeschooling was to avoid sending our oldest daughter to the middle school. Through the years the list of reasons has grown and become so much more than we could have ever imagined. Here are some of the top reasons we love to homeschool:

- Seeing the excitement when the "lightbulb" turns on
- Flexibility
- Creating a personalized education
- Making our own schedule
- Teaching through the lens of a Christian worldview
- Spending more time with dad
- Taking vacations in the off season
- Teaching our children to think for themselves
- Time for our children to pursue their own interests

As I reflect back on all of our years of schooling at home, one of my favorite memories is seeing the excitement when the lightbulb came on as my child understood a new concept. We homeschooled our oldest two daughters after they had spent a few years in public elementary school, but we have home-schooled our youngest daughter since kindergarten. We en-rolled her in a private Christian school for her 2nd grade year, but after one semester she wanted to come back to our home-school. She is now a high school senior, so I have had the privilege of teaching her for the past thirteen years. I have loved educating her from kindergarten all the way through high school. Seeing her face light up as she learned to read is one of my favorite memories. Witnessing first hand all of her excitement as she learned anything new was such fun. Having a front row seat to watch her successes is a true joy. Even witnessing her tackle her least favorite subjects is a blessing, debating with me on why she should discontinue her study of Latin has even been a blessing as she shows off her debate skills. She learned those too well! Since the older two girls came home in late elementary school, I gave their early learning to other teachers and consequently missed many of their 'aha moments' as they mastered the learning of new concepts. I do regret this but cannot dwell on it. I remember the glee in our youngest daughter's face as she learned to read, to tell time, to count money and to spell new words.

Other valuable reasons we homeschool are the blessings of flexibility and freedom. Flexibility and freedom are beautiful things! I remember when my girls were in public school and our schedule was dictated, the time we had to be present at the school and the time we could leave. I had to get permission for them to go to a doctor or dentist appointment. When the grand-parents from out of town visited, I had to get permission to pick up the girls early so they could spend time with their Nana and Popey or their Gran and Pop Pop. I ran the risk of an unexcused tardy if my children overslept. The evenings were filled with homework, after school activities, and preparing for the next day. We did not have much flexibility or freedom. Recently, my nephew who is in the 4th grade in a public school, had to complete a science project over Thanksgiving break! What part of that assignment says break? It was a stressful situation for him and his parents, as they had travel and family plans, and in the midst of it all had to fit in time to work on the science project.

In addition to the start of the day and the ending of the day being dictated to you, there are the time constraints in the evening of tackling the homework sent home by the teachers. When my children were still in public school, our evenings became consumed with homework as they entered upper elementary school, even 2nd and 3rd grades brought with them a significant amount of homework. We spent too much time in the evenings trying to get all of the work accomplished. After a full day in school, the last thing my kids wanted to do was sit at the kitchen table looking at more school work. For us, spelling homework was just busy work. For some reason my children have been great spellers with little effort. Writing spelling sentences and the words 10x each several nights a week was not something that spelled success for us. Our kids could have learned the elementary math without all of the math sheets for homework. They could master each skill with enough practice in math class during the school day. As a homeschool family we have the rule in our house of no assigned homework. The girls love to read and so evenings may be spent with some reading or researching something, but all of our classwork is done during the school day. Our motto has always been to work hard during the day, so we can play in the evenings. We love that we have the flexibility to make our own schedule that dictates when we will do our school work. We choose our own way, and that is freeing!

It was Socrates who said, "An unexamined life is not worth living." Are you examining your current situation? Maybe you too want more control of and more flexibility in your schedule.

Ask God to help you as you seek to honor Him and to do what is best for your family.

Proverbs 16:3 tells us,

> "Commit your works to the Lord, And your thoughts will be established."

Talk to God about your ideas and ask him to help you to implement them well.

Psalm 90:17 is a favorite Scripture of mine and a beautiful reminder of God helping us in our work,

> "And let the beauty of the Lord our God be upon us,
> And establish the work of our hands for us,
> Yes, establish the work of our hands."

The next reason on our list of reasons why we homeschool is that of creating a personalized education. In our homeschooling we love that we can use a wide variety of curriculum to teach to each child's strengths and personality. We can also choose curriculum that helps to strengthen weaknesses. Our middle daughter had comprehension issues, thus needing a curriculum that concentrated on comprehension. Our oldest daughter is the "everything came easy to her" type of learner. She received good grades with little effort. It was easy to choose a curriculum for her. Our middle daughter, on the other hand, struggled for every good grade she received. It took her extra time in learning anything new. I had to adapt her education to include extra comprehension helps. Our youngest daughter is a learner who truly delights in learning. She is the student, who once she learns about something and has taken the test to move on, still researches and reads about the subject. She always wants to learn more. It is hard to believe all three girls, who were raised in the same home, by the same two parents, in a relatively same school environment, could be so different. It speaks to the importance of personalizing a child's education. As homeschool parents we get to teach our students with extra helps in subjects in which they struggle, but we also get to take extra time to enjoy the subjects they love. My girls were all literature lovers and prolific writers. We enjoyed reading many books aloud together. We all remember my sobbing at the kitchen table as we read the extremely sad ending of *Where the Red Fern Grows*! Personalized education for each student cannot be done in an adequate fashion in a public school setting, with the average class size of 20+ students. When I taught in the public school system, I had middle school English classes of 30+ students. It is nearly impossible to individualize and personalize a child's learning when you have that many students of varying abilities in the same class. I have a grandson. He has a difficult time sitting still. He wants to be outside all the time. The instances when I help him with his schoolwork show me that I would have to teach him differently than I taught his mom and his aunts if I were to school him full time. A personalized education is beneficial to the child because it teaches to his strengths and helps with his weaknesses. It takes into account what will spark a child's interest and what will help him learn material most effectively.

Another reason our family homeschools is we can make our own schedule. We, not the school, have control of our schedule. This means that if one of our girls gets sick I do not have to call the school to get her make up work and get the school's permission for her to be excused. This also means that if we want to take a week off from school in the fall to go on vacation, we have the control to do just that. We do not have to worry if we will exceed the school system's number of accepted yearly absences.

You are in charge of making your daily schedule. You may have math and writing every day but history and electives every other day. For the upper grades, you may spend one morning a week on nothing but science and labs, or for a younger student you may choose instead to spend the morning outdoors observing nature for your science class. You can choose to have a weekday morning or afternoon where there is no organized classroom time. There are many possibilities. Our schedule looked different depending on the age of the girls. A kindergarten schedule is much different than a high school freshman schedule. The beauty is you get to determine your own schedule each year. Part of our scheduling process each school year is to have our daughters give input for our schedule. Children have great insight! I have appreciated their thoughts and ideas through the years.

Another reason on our list of reasons why we love to homeschool is the fact that I can teach my kids all of the school subjects through the lens of a Christian worldview. Everything that we study can be brought back to our Creator. We have been able to wrestle with such topics as creation vs. evolution, euthanasia, abortion, and other controversial topics as we look to God's Word. We have discussions which are seeking answers that are glorifying to Him. The *Classical Conversations* program that we have been involved with these past several years has the motto, "To know God and to make Him known". All subjects are taught through a Christian worldview.

Another reason why we love homeschooling is that the lifestyle allows us to schedule more dad time. We love spending as much time as possible with my husband. In the early days of homeschooling, we looked forward to his coming home for lunch. He presently works a different schedule, but we still like to meet him for lunch once a week. Being at home allows us to work around his schedule for time off to participate in hobbies and entertainment. He has been instrumental in helping me school the girls, and he schedules time each day to teach math as well as to answer any science questions. The girls' dad has been a vital part of our homeschool journey.

A definite perk on our list of why we love to homeschool is that we can take vacations during the off season. We are extremely spoiled in doing this. During the few times we have had to go on vacation during peak season, we have not enjoyed it nearly as much as those off season times with fewer crowds. There are homeschool discounts at many destinations. Great Wolf Lodge, various science museums and aquariums, Colonial Williamsburg, as well as many other historical sites are examples of places that have discounts for homeschoolers or specific days set aside just for homeschoolers. We have saved a lot of money on our vacations traveling in the off season. The beach is wonderful in May and October. The lines are much shorter at Great Wolf Lodge in the winter months on a Tuesday or Wednesday than on the weekends. We enjoy boating on Smith Mountain Lake. Saturdays and Sundays are full of boat traffic, but we love to go out on the weekdays when there are far fewer boats on the water. We are able to participate in many activities during the weekdays when there are fewer crowds. This is a definite perk, and one that makes our life less stressed.

Another important reason that makes our list is we teach our kids to ask questions and to think on their own. We choose curriculum that helps facilitate this thought process. *Apologia* science texts have been a favorite of ours. *Defeating Darwinism* by Phillip E. Johnson and *How Then Should We Live* by Francis Schaeffer have both been wonderful high school books for contemplating important issues. We read *Night* by Elie Wiesel, *The Diary of Anne Frank*, and the autobiography of Corrie Ten Boom, *The Hiding Place* to discuss the horrors of the Holocaust. We read *The Consequences of Ideas* by R. C. Sproul to study philosophy from the ancient world to the present day. Homeschool affords us the time to read about and discuss important issues.

My husband and I have taught our daughters to think for themselves and to ask questions. We encourage them to seek truth, looking at everything through the truth of God's Word, having them channel everything they hear to weigh it against what they know from God's Word. My greatest accomplishment with my youngest daughter was reading the Bible through in Its entirety. We started reading a chapter each school day starting sometime in her 4th grade year and in March of her 11th grade year we finished. My prayer journal entry for March 22, 2019 states, "Today my youngest and I read the last chapter of Ezekiel thus accomplishing our goal of reading the Bible through in Its entirety. What a blessing to us both. I think it is my greatest accomplishment as a mom, this sharing of the Scripture together. May our daughter hide God's Word in her heart forever.". Obviously, we did not start at Genesis and end with Revelation. We started with Psalms and Proverbs and then chose other Books until one day all we had left to read was Ezekiel.

The final reason on the list for why we love to homeschool is our kids have the time to explore what interests them. I desire to let my girls choose what they want to be involved in, allowing them the time to develop their own interests instead of pushing them into things that I think they should do. Together we intentionally seek out ideas or opportunities that have an eternal focus, maybe something God will use in His plan for them. We weigh if the activity will be beneficial to them. Sometimes the benefit is just pure fun. I try to model and to teach them to self-examine their choices. We see the fruits and the blessings of this. Our kids have been able to pursue varied interests. As previously mentioned, our oldest took quilting classes and learned to quilt. She worked two days a week at the local quilt shop during her early high school years. She has made beautiful quilts and has been able to use her sewing skills in various ways. She also spent a lot of time with horses, attending summer horse camps, and having a horse of her own. I see her love of animals shining through into her adulthood. She still loves horses, and at this present time lives on a horse farm. At the end of her junior year of high school, she gained employment at the local radio station as an on-air announcer. Because of her experience with this job, in addition to her love for what she was doing, she decided to major in communications at *Liberty University* in Lynchburg, Virginia. We saw God's hand in the entire process. In the fall of 2008, during her senior year in high school, she entered a scholarship contest along with approximately 200 other area high school juniors and seniors. The contest was sponsored by an area Christian radio station and also by *Liberty University*. The grand prize winner would receive a full tuition scholarship. Our daughter was chosen in the first round of applicants, then again in the second round, finally receiving the phone call that she was one of the top three finalists. She had several radio and newspaper interviews. The radio interviews came naturally to her, since she was already a radio announcer, giving her a definite advantage. She ended up winning the scholarship. Being part of a homeschool family opened up so many opportunities for her.

Our middle daughter pursued a role in any and every play for which she could audition during her middle and high school years. Theatre was definitely her love, and she wanted to do nothing but perform. Homeschooling allowed her the time to pursue this interest.

Both girls have since graduated from college. Our oldest was a communications major at Liberty University, with an emphasis in both radio and television. She was a television news reporter for four years and now has her own social media business, as well as her real estate license. Our middle daughter has a fine arts degree with an emphasis in theatre from Milligan University. She is active in local community theatre and is an ophthalmologist assistant. We tease her that she has to have her day job to fund her love of all things theatre!

Our youngest daughter has been able to pursue her passion for playing the violin. Being homeschooled is a huge benefit for her musically, because every Tuesday we travel several hours for her to take violin lessons at the University of North Carolina. She also practices on her violin two to three hours a day. There would not be enough hours in the week for her if she had to adhere to a public school schedule. She plans to attend Liberty University in the fall to major in violin performance. She has been able to play in the local youth symphony, in local churches and attend many summer music camps. What began as a music education project for her at a local university turned into much more than any of us could ever imagine. Each of our girls were able to take the time to explore what interested them and found their life's passion as a result.

We rested in the knowledge that all of our reasons to home-school put us on the right path for our family. I had to remind myself more often at the beginning of our journey that what we had chosen was the right choice for our family. People tend to voice their opinions and comment on homeschooling when they have no idea what we do. I have had total strangers give me reasons why I am doing a disservice to my kids by teaching them at home. To be fair I have also had good conversations with strangers about homeschooling but as a homeschool family, I am sorry to say, you will not be exempt from negative conversations and questions. Here are a few that my husband, my children and I have been asked:

How will your children fare in college?

How can they even go to college without public school transcripts?

What about the SOL tests?

How will they be socialized?

What about sports and school clubs?

Do you stay in your pajamas all day?

Do you sleep late?

How can you teach all of the subjects?

Do you have a teaching degree?

Do your kids like it?

How can you stay home all day, every day?

What do you do for gym class credit?

These questions use to really bother me. Often they are asked quite rudely. The title of this book came from an interaction between our youngest daughter and an elderly woman. It is an interaction that sums up the topic of rude questioning. Our daughter went to a retirement home to play her violin for the residents living there. After she played her musical selections there was a question and answer time. The audience members asked her several questions to which she gave answers. As the Q and A time was ending one woman sitting in the front row asked, "Where do you go to school?" to which Mary Ruth responded, "I am homeschooled." The woman looked at her and said, (cue grouchy old lady voice) "Eww....you homeschool. Do you like it?" Mary Ruth responded that she did. The woman scrunched up her face and repeated Eww! We laugh about it now, but initially it was not as funny. Yes, we homeschool; and yes, we love it!

I handle rude questions more easily these days; I try to give informed answers hoping the skeptics will get the hint that I know what I am doing. I have gained confidence throughout the past 18 years and have learned to not care so much about what others think. I know I do a good job, and I know I am doing what is best for our family. Our daughters are successful and happy adults. They excelled in college. Who cares about those stupid SOL tests! Socialization.... are you kidding me? Our oldest daughter was a television news reporter and is now an entrepreneur with her own social media business. Our middle daughter was a theatre major and performs often in our community theater. Our youngest loves public speaking and plays the violin in front of hundreds of people. I would say that they are definitely "socialized". They grew up learning to get along with each other and with me and their dad. If we cannot learn to get along within our own family, how can we expect to get along with the outside world? Our kids were part of peer groups that were fun and where all of the young people felt they could be themselves. I loved this about their homeschool friends, they were unique because they were not pressured to be like everyone else. My oldest daughter's friend group was the best example of this. There were ten kids in the group and no two were alike. They were all the best of friends, and a beautiful example of inclusiveness and acceptance.

Guess what? Even if my children were not as outgoing as they are, they would still be able to excel in society. They have been taught who they are in Christ Jesus, and the value this truth brings. I do not want them to be like the world, to be like everyone else. I want them to be "free to be you and me" personalities. Our kids say, "Our family is so weird." There is nothing wrong with weird. What I never want them to be is a person who does not think outside of the box or someone who feels as if she has to fit a certain mold. I had to often remind myself at the beginning of my journey that I was doing the right thing and that the girls would be O.K. Now, in hindsight I KNOW they are more than O.K.

In our homeschool God is faithful. He has proven Ephesians 3:20 to us over and over again, "Now to Him who is able to do exceedingly abundantly above all that we ask or think, according to the power that works in us." My confidence in my homeschool success is not rooted in how others view me and our decision to homeschool. This makes the negative, snarky questions much easier to ignore. My success is not rooted in myself or in anything that we have done, but in God's sovereign power. I love the promise in Psalm 32:8, "I will instruct you and teach you in the way you should go; I will guide you with My eye." God helps me see the way I need to go and keeps His loving eye on me as I do it. My husband, our girls, and I are confident in what we do and have a long list of reasons for why we love what we do. I look at our girls, at our conversations, at our memories, at our life, and know what we are doing is the very best for our family.

CHAPTER 4

Goal Setting, Scheduling and Tips for Discipline

As you begin your homeschool journey, you will need to make a list of goals. Separate your goals into yearly, monthly, and daily lists. Write down a goal list for you personally and also one for each of your children as well. Your goals will vary by school year. When our youngest was in kindergarten my goal was to teach her for half of the day. We were always finished by lunch leaving her afternoon for playtime. I wanted her to know her days of the week, months of the year, start on basic math concepts (she had a paperback *Dora the Explorer* math book), and practice reading and writing. In contrast, for her junior year in high school, our goals were to work hard both morning and afternoon, learning Advanced Math, reading about early philosophers, participating in debate, writing well executed essays, reading and discussing five Shakespeare plays, studying Chemistry and conducting lab experiments, and studying United States history. I had continuing her Latin study as one of my goals, but she debated good reasons why three years of Latin study was sufficient. Her debate class has trained her well! Your goal setting should be specific and measurable. It is difficult for a child to meet the expectations you have for him if he does not know what you want him to do. Make the goals as specific as possible and share with your students how you plan to measure the success of their goal achievement. Communication of these expectations and goals is vital in keeping everyone on track. Revisit your goal lists periodically to help to maintain accountability. I begin each school year with a goal setting session. I write what I hope to accomplish in the upcoming school year. I pray about all of my ideas and share them with our daughter who is now the only one still at home. She knows what her father and I expect of her for the upcoming school year. We listen to her as she shares her goals for the year. She enjoys making her yearly goal list. It is beneficial to look back at what we wrote as the year progresses. We have fun seeing the end results. Some goals are checked off and some, for various reasons, are left undone. It is a system of checks and balances for us. I did not do as much goal setting with my older girls and regret that we did not. Time and experience teach a lot of lessons, and I realized with our youngest daughter this is an insightful and enjoyable task for the start of our school year. These goal setting sessions help ensure we are all on the same page. You can tailor this to your unique situation. I know some kids enjoy doing things like this better than others. My grandson, for instance, would not enjoy sitting down for my goal setting session or making his own goal list. I would have to change how I conduct this activity, brainstorming ideas orally with him and writing them on a poster board that we would display in our classroom. He likes typing on the computer, so I could incorporate this to help him write out his goals. I know creative and crafty people who have made beautiful artwork showcasing their yearly, monthly, and weekly goals. We can all adopt ideas that work for our family goal setting.

Another aspect to consider when homeschooling is scheduling. A 180 day school year is pretty normal and works out to four 9 – week quarters, two 18 – week semesters, or 36 weeks. Most homeschool curriculum publishers base their products on this 36 week model. Jessica Parnell, CEO of Edovate Learning Corp and the homeschooling program Bridgeway Academy gives these guidelines for the recommended hours per day to homeschool, "We recommend that true homeschoolers spend about an hour to two hours a day for the elementary years, two to three hours a day for the middle school years, and three to four hours a day for the high school years." Our family spent more time than this in later elementary and middle school years, but this information is a good starting point.

Remember, there is a lot of wasted time in a public school day. We eliminate this waste of time in our school room. There is no waiting for the rest of the class to finish the designated school work, no waiting for the teacher to reprimand the misbehaving student and no need to interrupt learning to refocus multiple students. Our daughters were always waiting in their public elementary school classrooms to start the next subject, as they finished their assignments relatively quickly. Thus in our homeschool they enjoyed being able to start a new subject as soon as they were ready, not having to wait until other students were ready as well. This saved a lot of time. Some families choose to homeschool three days a week and use the other two days for chores, errands, appointments, or field trips. Families may choose to take Monday or Friday off in order to have a fieldtrip or family fun day. I know several families who keep Friday free so that they have the flexibility of three day weekends. This is helpful when you have family who live out of town, coming in to visit for a 3 day weekend, as well as when you travel to visit them for a long weekend.

Thoughtco.com gives this list of six tips for creating a daily homeschool schedule:

1. Create a routine, not a schedule
2. Work in chunks
3. Leave some margin
4. Schedule each sibling
5. Do not try to do every subject every day
6. Follow your natural inclinations

You will have to figure out a schedule that works for your family. We tackled the subjects that we had a more difficult time with in the morning. We began our days Monday – Friday at approximately 8:45 with Bible study and prayer first thing and then moved on to our core subjects (Math, Science, Language Arts) for the remainder of the morning. We always had math first and science next. We usually had time to fit in one more class before lunch, which depending on the school year was either spelling and reading or language and grammar. We had a break from 11:30 – 1:00 for lunch and free time. We had elective classes and social studies/ history in the afternoon. English is my love and all of the girls enjoy it as well, so we spent time each day reading great short stories, poetry and classics. Reading was often done outside of our normal school day schedule. For example, I know families whose father reads them a chapter a night from classic literature. Our girls read on their own each night before bedtime. One of my favorite pictures that I took of them is when they were ages 14, 11, and 2 years of age, and they were all in the oldest sister's bed each one reading her own book. I can see from the picture that the oldest is reading Shakespeare! What a treasured moment in time captured for all to enjoy!

One of the many benefits of homeschooling is that you can decide what schedule best suits your family. If dad is off on

Wednesdays perhaps that will be a day off in your school week. We periodically take a half or full day off. It gives us all a much needed break from our set schedule. We are disciplined in our family. It is in our DNA. With that said however, we do seem to start school later and later as the end of the year approaches. We may start out in August at 8:30/8:45, but by April we are lucky to start by 9:30. We also become a little slack in our assignments. It is a joke with the girls, because if they ask me during first semester if they can skip something or do every other math problem the answer is no, but if they ask me in March or April they know the answer is more often than not a yes. This is another blessing of dictating your schedule, allowing for flexibility and change. The key is to goal set, figure out what works for you and your kids, and be flexible without endangering the quality of your child's education. It takes time to figure out the healthy balance. There is a place for hard work and a place for play. In all that we do, we want to educate them well, and to do all for the glory of God.

I have friends who do not have a set schedule. It works for some and quite frankly it does not work for others. You should be able to maintain a schedule that gives you an end result of a definite start date and finish date for your school day, as well as for your school year. I know families who homeschool year round. That is their chosen schedule, and although my kids and I would hate to school in the summer, it does work for some. What does not work is when a family is never finishing work on time and getting further and further behind because of no set schedule or the discipline to adhere to set goals. This is a recipe for disaster and is one of the biggest causes of burnout for both mother and student. It is frustrating for everyone when work is not done diligently during the day, the result being endless evenings and weekends of frustration trying to dig out of the pit of falling behind. We worked diligently on a daily weekday schedule so that we could play in the evenings and on the weekends. We started our school year at the end of August and finished by the end of May. This gave my girls the goal of finishing the school year by the middle to the end of May. Then they could enjoy all of June, July and most of August for their summer break. We all looked forward to our break! With that goal in the forefront of our minds, we worked hard. We also have scheduled Thanksgiving, Christmas, and Easter breaks. Just as taking a daily lunch/free time break is beneficial to our minds, so is taking these extended breaks. We return from a break feeling refreshed and sometimes even excited and ready!

What does a typical day look like? Some days are anything but typical, but here is a glimpse of a typical day for us. I am sharing two different snapshots, one when I schooled all three of our girls and the next one when only schooling one child:

Schedule with all Three Girls (School levels: High school, Middle school, and Elementary school)

- 7:30 am: wakeup and breakfast time
- 8:30 am: devotional time
- 8:45 am: older two girls start math with their Dad, and the youngest begins schoolwork with me
- 10:00 am: older two girls work on science, youngest continues work with me
- 11:00 am: older two girls work on history/social studies, youngest finishes school work for the day
- 12:00 - 1:30 pm: lunch break/free time
- 1:30 pm: I check morning work; we discuss any questions. Older girls work on writing and grammar with me, youngest plays (until 3rd grade, when she too schooled in the afternoon)
- 3:00 pm: wrap up the school day, and spend the rest of the afternoon reading and physical education

Schedule with One Child (High school- 9th grade)

- 8:30 am: wakeup and breakfast
- 9:00 am: devotional time
- 9:15 am: Math
- 10:15 am: Latin
- 11:15 am: Science
- 12:00 - 1:00 pm: lunch and free time
- 1:00 pm: Writing and Literature
- 2:00 pm: History, Debate
- 3:00 pm: wrap up school day

Starting each day at the same time has always kept us on track. Devotions were a priority and have helped our days go more smoothly. I encourage you to do the same; you will see the results! Again, we always tackle the harder subjects in the morning when we are the freshest. I look at each school assignment every day. Some assignments were not graded, but I always checked each one. Keeping up with grades is important, especially for high school. You can find online forms to keep track of grades or you may choose to record them in a notebook by subject. I averaged grades every nine weeks. This made it easier to compute a final grade for the school year. It is best to record and average grades each 6 or 9 weeks, rather than trying to gather all of the grades from the entire school year to average.

Make sure cell phones and disruptions are put away during instruction time. We made it a point to not answer the phone during school hours. This set a precedent with family and friends that we were only available to talk during our lunch break or after school was dismissed for the day.

Time for physical education is important to schedule into your day. In our family we swim, hike, bike and walk. Just as you need to be aware of each child's specific interests in academics, be aware of his interests in exercise as well. Our oldest liked to take dance lessons and swim for exercise. Our middle daughter liked to bike and swim for exercise. Our youngest enjoys yoga, swimming and walking for her exercise. Sometimes my girls remember things differently than I do. For example, all three still talk about how I "forced" them to run around the house for exercise. Our youngest still moans about our morning routine of jumping jacks and sit ups. They are no worse for wear! I want them to be healthy and fit. Through these efforts of showing them from an early age the importance of fitness, they now continue to live healthy life styles.

Scheduling of classwork changes each year and there are big changes from elementary school to high school. We started with a few hours each day and my planning out everything. High school has a different story. Each year the course and work load change. In the early years of high school, I planned out each day and was involved with all of my daughters' subjects. When our youngest became a junior, she took over the planning and execution of her schedule. Each day is different, and she is in charge of her own work. She always makes sure that all of her work is completed for the week. She schedules her school day to allow herself ample violin practice time. This passing of the responsibility of scheduling to her was a big step for me. We once watched a movie where a girl described her mother as a Raptor bird vigilantly guarding her baby chick. My daughter fondly calls me Mother Raptor, for I am like a Raptor bird guarding her baby chick. I know parents who let their younger children be in charge of their school work schedule and who let them fend for themselves. They think they are preparing them for college, but all I witness is their children floundering. I encourage you to help your children, work alongside them, and teach them the best ways to organize and schedule in their early high school years. Your guidance and help will keep them on track and give them the support to not feel so overwhelmed. There will be a time in the later high school years for them to successfully take over. There will come a time to be less of a Mother Raptor!

Each year I get excited to begin the first day of school! When I think about it, I have spent my entire life since the age of five returning to school each fall. That is a lot of years "going back to school"! There was the exception of a few years when the first two girls were toddlers, but for the majority of my life fall means back to school. I try to make the first day a big deal. Here is my list of ideas for the first day of school:

1. Have a small first day of school gift. Some things I have given are a journal, pencils/pens, candy, pencil pouch, book by a favorite author, or a $5.00 gift card.
2. Look through all of your textbooks with your child. I remember the year when we were half way through the school year when we realized there was important information and helps in the back of the textbook.
3. Have lunch outside.
4. Start a read aloud.
5. Have a first day of school activity. I find neat ideas on the internet.
6. Have your child write out his goals and what he hopes to accomplish during the school year.
7. Use music, art, or a game in your lesson plans.
8. Pray often and together.
9. Give yourself grace.
10. Pace yourself.
11. Remember, "Play is the highest form of research." – Albert Einstein

Each family's school day looks different. Each schoolroom looks different. We had school at the kitchen table. I had a "school closet" and we would get our books out every morning and put them back each afternoon. It is nice for those of you who have an actual schoolroom where you can hang posters, maps, dry erase boards, etc. I had friends who had school desks, bulletin boards, and chalk boards. I think this is all great, but we were just as happy at our kitchen table. We liked pulling school out and then putting it all away. I am not the most creative person, so this eliminated the need to decorate a classroom. There were times when I did wish I could leave everything out on a desk, have a book case to store books, and have cabinets to store supplies, but we were never in a home with the extra room. Whatever your school room situation is like, make it work for you. I like the following from the Facebook page *Wooden Spoons and Brown Paper*: "An open letter to the new homeschool parents: Proceed with caution, sweet newcomer. Pinterest is going to try to fool you. Pinterest is desperately going to try to convince you what your homeschool ought to look like. But may I let you in on a little secret? Pinterest doesn't make the rules. No two homeschool journeys are alike. And though you may be tempted to feel discouraged that yours isn't Pinterest perfect or "just so"... remember that the only thing important is that it's perfect for you."

Remember that our goal as homeschool parents should be to raise up children who are well – rounded individuals who think for themselves and who live for Christ. The schedule and classroom environment are important, but not the most important.

Homeschool Helps

If you are concerned about teaching certain subjects, you are not alone. None of us knows every subject at a mastery level. Here are some ideas for help with various subjects:

- Math is **not** my love. I have roughly an Algebra 1 level of understanding, definitely not a mastery level to teach higher math courses. My husband, on the other hand, does enjoy math and has a background in and an understanding of higher level concepts. He has always been a vital part of our homeschool math class. He took over teaching for me when the girls started Algebra 1. He taught Algebra, Geometry, Advanced Math and Calculus to the girls. Perhaps your husband, sister, friend, neighbor, etc. could take over this subject for you. I know families who have the blessing of grandparents living nearby who help teach math. Area colleges offer math camps in the summer. Hiring a math tutor may be your answer. Tutors charge anywhere from $10.00 to $80.00 an hour. There are also tutoring web sites such as *Wyzant* and *Tutor.com* that can help your student conquer math concepts.

- I also needed assistance with science. When the older two girls needed high school sciences we were part of an amazing co-op where Physical Science, Chemistry and Biology were taught by women and men who had science degrees and a love for the subject. I believe that as homeschool teachers we do not have to have a degree to teach many things, but in our family we did want this for the high school sciences. The kids needed the concepts taught more in depth than I was able to teach them, and we wanted them to have labs in a group setting. I personally did not want to order the earth worm, cow eye, frog, and pig to conduct the dissection at our kitchen table! Many colleges have science camps and homeschool science days. Check the colleges in your area to see what is available. Ask your homeschool friends if they want to get together as a group to conduct the science labs together. You can also hire a science tutor.
- You may need help with a foreign language study. There are video programs available. In these programs your

child is part of a virtual classroom, seeing the instruction given as well as being able to ask questions. There are tutorials available on the internet, many are found on *YouTube*. We found several to help us understand Latin grammar. LatinPerDiem, a free tutorial just a google away, gives daily Latin lessons in four minutes or less.

- If you live near a College or University call the departments you are interested in and ask if they have programs your child can attend. We have participated in several math, science, and music programs at area universities. Our daughter was able to enroll in a science fair competition at a nearby university. There are lots of options out there; you just have to look for them.

Sometimes one of the reasons people think they cannot homeschool, feeling inadequate, is because they do not have a college degree or specifically a teaching certificate. I have a Bachelor of Arts in English and a Secondary Education degree, with a certified Virginia teaching license. I will admit this has helped me in myriad ways such as in my planning, execution, and classroom expectations. But at the same time this has been a hindrance because of my initial ideas of extreme structure, lack of creativity, and the need to teach to the textbook. The beauty of homeschooling is that we learn alongside our child. I have learned more through the years teaching all of the subjects to my kids than I ever knew before. Sound curriculum comes with workable teacher guides and teacher helps. You can teach your child! It bothers me that often when people accept our homeschooling as a public school alternative, it is because they learn I was once a public school teacher. People think my education degree, as well as my past in a public school classroom, validates our decision. I know many great home school parents who do not have teaching degrees. Some do not have a college degree. They have a passion and desire to teach their children well. The passion and desire to teach well is far more important than the college education. Have the passion and desire to be the best learner alongside your child that you can possibly be.

"Myth: Most homeschooling parents are not academically qualified to teach their children.

Reality: Studies show that homeschool students score above average on achievement tests regardless of their parents' level of formal education. It turns out that it isn't the "smarts" of the parents that matters most, but their commitment to helping their children learn." Source: www.nheri.org

What about Discipline?
We Can't Send our Students to the Principal!

Let's face it, there are hard days in a homeschool setting, just as there are hard days in any environment. You have to learn through trial and error the best ways to incorporate expectations and discipline, which can be difficult as you play both the role of the mother and the teacher. Sometimes these two lines cross, intersect, or collide. It takes time and discernment to figure out the balance. I did not do a good job with this in the early years. I am much more comfortable in my various roles today, much of the reason being the experiences and time I have had to flesh out what works and what does not. When the going gets tough, we are not able to walk away. We cannot send students to the principal or call parents to complain about their child's discipline problem. We are that parent, and as such we have to deal with it. I am a flight person. Research shows that there are two types of people, those who fight when the going gets tough and those who run. I tend to run; I retreat to a corner when there is a problem or a conflict. I do not do well with conflicts, disagreements, blood; they make me uncomfortable. I know why I do not have a house full of boys. My grandson is a daredevil. He comes to me periodically with blood dripping from some wounded part of his body. I immediately yell for my husband or my daughter. I am a flight person. As hard as I try not to be, this is my initial response. Some people face problems head on. I circle around them multiple times and then try to sneak out the back door! I want everything to run smoothly and everyone to be happy. This has made it harder for me to discipline my children, meeting our classroom problems head on. I am a work in progress!

Since we cannot get away from our students, except for those few minutes when we lock ourselves in the bathroom, we have to be creative in ways to refresh and refocus. We have to give our children both boundaries and rules. We have to decide on a discipline plan that works for our families. Perhaps you do send your child to the principal if you are a family who has the father as the principal. I have seen that work well. We do not get to wave goodbye every morning as we put our kids on the bus, so we have to pace our day. This pacing was one of the hardest things for me to conquer. Discipline has also been one of the hardest aspects of homeschooling for me. I have failed more in this than I care to admit.

Proverbs has a lot to say about the topic of discipline. Here are several Scriptures to encourage you to make and keep a school discipline plan:

- Proverbs 25:28 states, "Whoever has no rule over his own spirit is like a city broken down, without walls."
- Proverbs 3:11-13 states, "My son do not despise the chastening of the Lord, nor detest his correction; For whom the Lord loves He corrects, Just as a father the son in whom he delights."
- Proverbs 19:18 informs us to "Chasten your son while there is hope, And do not set your heart on his destruction."

- Proverbs 15:5 declares, "A fool despises his father's instruction, But he who receives correction is prudent."
- Proverbs 19:8 asserts, "He who gets wisdom loves his own soul; He who keeps understanding will find good."
- Proverbs 8: 32-35 tells us how blessed we are to keep God's ways in order to gain wisdom, "Now therefore listen to me, my children for blessed are those who keep my ways. Hear instruction and be wise, and do not disdain it. Blessed is the man that listens to me, watching daily at my gates, waiting at the posts of my doors."
- Proverbs 13:24 states, "He who spares his rod hates his son, But he who loves him disciplines him promptly."

Wow, that is a lot of Scriptures speaking to the importance of discipline. We will do well to heed this advice. It is important to have rules. A good idea is to write out a set of classroom rules. It is valuable to let your children know what is expected, what they can and cannot do. Children need clear boundaries. I encourage you to make a set of rules and to stick with them. If something makes you angry one day, but the next you say nothing about it how will your child be able to discern if it is a rule or not? I have learned that I need to enforce rules in our daily life. I will tell you it took me, a real people pleaser, quite a bit of time to realize this truth. My husband has been a huge help to me in this area. I have been caught trying to make the silliest request a reality for one of our girls, just to hear him say, "Stefanie, the answer needs to be no!" This may sound so simple, but believe me I need to hear this quite often. What happens is that I tend to "bend over backwards" so much that I get frazzled and frustrated and end up in a place that is not pretty. Maybe some of you can relate. For those of you who are better with boundaries, good for you!

In your classroom concentrate on the positives and praise good behavior. Focusing on negative behavior will not accomplish anything but your child tuning you out. I made it a point to concentrate on the positives. I would say things like, "Wow, your desk looks organized." and "Thanks for getting the clothes out of the dryer before I asked you to do it." My favorite was to catch the girls being kind to each other, since that was more difficult to witness. An example of this is, "What a kind way to treat your sister, I bet that made her feel special." Something so simple is quite effective. With this approach, the tone in our home is a more pleasant one. I may not always find the desk or the treatment of a sister worthy of praise, but I do see more positive results when I am looking for ways to praise the girls. Try it with your students. Being positive will help you have a much happier school environment.

To help stay positive you will need to find ways to gain peace throughout your day. A homeschool day can seem to drag on forever at times. I remember some particularly long days! I am a hot tea drinker. Tea relaxes me, and it makes me feel like I am taking the time to do something just for me. It is a seemingly little thing, but is a big one when it comes to helping my state of mind. Make your own self-care habits. I do not particularly like the word self-care when defined as putting oneself first, but I do believe that in the midst of caring for everyone else you need to have special intentional habits for your well-being.

When my girls were younger, I sent them to their rooms for a set time each afternoon so I could have some alone time, as "alone" as I could get during those days. When our youngest was born and we had such different ages in the house it became a balancing act to gain any alone time. When the youngest started Kindergarten I was schooling a middle school and a high school student as well. Some of you have several children, teaching varied ages. It can certainly be done, but it takes a lot of juggling. Remember, in the midst of it all to choose something you enjoy doing to give you some daily refreshment. It may be exercising, reading, praying, hiding for a few minutes, or enjoying a cup of coffee/tea.

Disciplining a child is very important; teaching a child to respect authority will teach them to respect God and His Word. Adhering to the rules in your household will go a long way in your being able to enjoy your children. We must fight against wanting to make excuses for our children, and teach them the meaning of consequences. In 1 Samuel the high priest Eli looked the other way when his sons blatantly disobeyed. We are not given a glimpse of the father he was when the boys were young, but as grown men he chose to ignore their selfish, lustful, and rebellious behavior. Maybe he hoped that by ignoring the behavior it eventually would go away. We may be tempted to think the same thing, but we all know ignoring bad behavior does not make it go away. Eli learned this lesson the hard way. In 1 Samuel 2:29 God asks Eli, "Why do you kick at my sacrifice and my offering which I have commanded in my dwelling place, and honor your sons more than me, to make yourselves fat with the best of all the offerings of Israel my people?" Eli did not discipline his sons. He should have removed them from service in the temple as a consequence for their bad behavior. The Lord told Eli in 1 Samuel 2:34 and 1 Samuel 4:17-18 that the family would suffer judgment because of his sons' behavior and his allowance of such behavior. As Christian parents we have the huge responsibility to lovingly discipline our children. Hebrews 12:7-11 clearly tells us, "If you endure chastening, God deals with you as with sons; for what son is there whom a father does not chasten? But if you are without chastening, of which all have become partakers, then you are illegitimate and not sons. Furthermore, we have had human fathers who corrected us, and we paid them respect. Shall we not much more readily be in subjection to the Father of spirits and live? For they indeed for a few days chastened us as seemed best to them, but He for our profit, that we may be partakers of His holiness.

Now no chastening seems to be joyful for the present, but painful; nevertheless, afterward it yields the peaceable fruit of righteousness to those who have been trained by it." We desire the end result of discipline, which is helping our children develop into responsible, God-fearing adults who are obedient to God's Word.

CHAPTER 5

Prayer, a Parent's Influence, and the Measure of Success

O ur homeschool story started with prayer. Long before I was researching and reaching out about all things homeschool, I was seeking an answer from God about what to do for our daughters' educations. This time of prayer happened before homeschool ever took root in my heart. God was preparing me in many ways, ways I can now see only in hindsight. I understand the way in which many prayers were answered. I know that even when I was praying about whether to continue sending our kids to public school or making a change and sending them to a private Christian school, the idea of homeschooling was a tiny seed starting to grow. Prayer is a vital part of a Christian's life. Oswald Chambers reminds us, "Prayer is the place where God puts His soldiers, clad in armour, and indwelt by His Spirit."[2] Pray about what is on your heart, sharing your hopes, concerns, and dreams with our Heavenly Father. Talk to him about your heart's desires, your plans, and your ideas.

---

2. Taken from *If Ye Shall Ask* by Oswald Chambers 1937 by Oswald Chambers Publications Association Ltd. Used by permission of Our Daily Bread Publishing, Box 3566, Grand Rapids, MI 49501. All rights reserved.

As I reflect back over the years, I definitely would have prayed more if I could have a "do over". Our third child has witnessed much better schooling than our older two, for I have learned to take more time to pray. I have also learned that my passion for praying God's will has grown as my walk with the Lord has grown. I realize that as I study God's Word, grow in my faith, and live out God's Word in my daily life, I have a better chance of having the right attitude in my prayer life. I see that my obedience to God goes hand in hand with my prayers being more effective ones. Also, I see that my fervent prayer in all aspects of life correlate to my daily peace of mind and my joy in the Lord. This peace and joy from the Lord spills over into my homeschool classroom and naturally into the students who are part of it. George Mueller, Christian evangelist and missionary, said, "The vigor of our spiritual life will be in exact proportion to the place held by the Bible in our life and thoughts." He also stated, "The first great and primary business to which I ought to attend every day is to have my soul happy in the Lord."

I want to encourage you to daily take the time to pray about your school situation. Ask God to give you the help and strength to do what needs to be done. Ask for a discerning heart. Do not be deceived; it takes hard work and effort to be an effective homeschool teacher. Effective is the key word. There are examples of poor homeschooling, but there are also many examples of excellent homeschooling. Being a home educator who excels in her classroom takes perseverance and hard work, even on those days when you do not feel like doing it. Our youngest daughter feels like skipping her math lesson on a pretty much daily basis, yet she continues to persevere. She has to continue on, or she will be doing math all summer long! She and I both acknowledge that prayer gives us the discipline and strength to persevere. Praying for this discipline and strength has helped us get through many a school lesson. Take each day at a time and know that God gives you what you need for that day. Keep your focus to do the hard work one day at a time. Before you know it that one day turns into many days, and you are finishing an entire school year where you and your kids have persevered, all with God's help.

Intentionality in prayer is a foundation for any school day effectiveness, for without God's help we will ultimately fail. Your homeschooling success will be a result of such intentional prayer. I hope you realize that without focused prayer you will not be successful in what God has for you and for your children. Ask godly friends, family and others with whom you associate to pray for you. It is always a good idea to have an accountability partner; a fellow homeschool mom is a great choice to share life with you.

Proverbs 24:10 comes to my mind when I think about the homeschooling of my children, "If you faint in the day of adversity, Your strength is small." There will be some adversity in the schooling of your children, but for strength to not be small it needs to come from God. Friends and family can uplift you and intercede for you. I praise God for my prayer warriors, for these dear ones I am grateful.

I daily pray for the wisdom and the strength to educate my children well. I acknowledge the fact that without God's help I would mess up everything. I am disappointed when I have missed a prayer opportunity and failed to sit down with one of the kids to lay everything out before the Lord. I am thankful that in God's mercy and grace He takes my failures and brings about good. He knows that my intense heart's desire is to do a job that is glorifying to Him. I believe this is key; He knows my heart's desire is to be a good and faithful servant in the raising and the schooling of the children He has entrusted to me.

When our family began homeschooling back in the early 2000's, I am ashamed to admit that I did not start the day with prayer. I was only focused on what school work needed to be accomplished, and we spent the entire school day crazed about working on and completing every lesson. I was determined to teach the entire textbook in every subject by the end of the school year. I can look back now and see the problems we had were, for the most part, due to that lack of prayer. My oldest still jokes about our first year of homeschooling, she being the guinea pig and all that she had to endure with my structure, ideas, and mess ups. It certainly was not a joke to her at the time, but years later in hind sight thankfully we are able to laugh about it. After much trial and error I realized prayer was a key ingredient missing from our day. Once we started to pray together the transformation was amazing! Everything was more enjoyable. Prayer certainly adds a brighter perspective to the day. It allows me to focus on what is really important and to not be so uptight about finishing every lesson in every textbook! What a difference I see in our attitudes as well. Having a God focus gives us more of a servant's heart in our interactions with each other. **Prayer** is a major key to success. Always give it a place of importance in your family's school day.

I love old hymns, and *Sweet Hour of Prayer* is one of my favorites,

"Sweet hour of prayer, sweet hour of prayer that calls me from a world of care, and bids me at my Father's Throne make all my wants and wishes known."[3]

Are you having sweet hours of prayer? Are you taking a break from this world of care to sit at our Father's Throne? Your spouse and your children are certainly worth the time and the effort. If we could truly grasp the eternal significance of prayer, we would spend **most** of our time talking to our Heavenly Father. Think of your time in prayer to be as vital as taking your next breath.

May we take the time to cherish Scripture, delighting in God's Word. May we daily find a healthy balance in our worship, work,

---

3. Walford, William, Sweet Hour of Prayer. New York: the New York Observer, 1845.

rest and play. May we live in contentment and thankfulness for the life God has given to us. This is my prayer for all of us.

I enjoy reading Oswald Chambers' book *Not Knowing Wither*. In a thought about intercession he writes, "The meaning of intercession is that we see what God is doing, consequently there is an intimacy between the child and Father which is never impertinent. We must pour into the bosom of God the cares which give us pain and anxiety in order that He may solve for us, and before us, the difficulties which we cannot solve. We injure our spiritual life when we dump the whole thing down before God and say— You do it. That spirit is blind to the real union with God. We must dump ourselves down in the midst of our problems and watch God solve them for us. 'But I have no faith'— Bring your problems to God and stay with Him while He solves them, then God Himself and the solution of your problems will be forever your own... If we could see the floor of God's immediate presence, we would find it strewn with the toys of God's children who have said— This is broken, I can't play with it anymore please give me another present. Only one in a thousand sits down in the midst of it all and says—I will watch my Father mend this."[4]

Let us be that one in a thousand! We, as homeschool families are in the midst of this very idea each day! We are living out our days sitting in our Father's midst asking for His help and His guidance. Our children witness this awesome interaction, and what a difference it makes!

The Influence of a Godly Parent

Deuteronomy 6:6-9 tells us, "And these words which I command you today shall be in your heart. You shall teach them

---

4. Taken from *Not Knowing Wither* by Oswald Chambers 1934 by Oswald Chambers Publications Association Ltd. Used by permission of Our Daily Bread Publishing, Box 3566, Grand Rapids, MI 49501. All rights reserved.

diligently to your children, and shall talk of them when you sit in your house, when you walk by the way, when you lie down, and when you rise up. You shall bind them as a sign on your hand, and they shall be as frontlets between your eyes. You shall write them on the door posts of your house and on your gates."

What does your child see when he looks at you? Are you diligently living God's ways in front of your child? John Newton, author of *Amazing Grace* said, "It is hard to shake off the influence of a Godly mother." God's intention is for a family to teach their children about the Lord. Is your influence that of a Godly parent? As a homeschool parent, you have the special opportunity of being able to choose your child's curriculum and the awesome opportunity of having time to delve into deep conversations with him. You have the opportunity to start each day with daily Bible reading. You have the ability to look at all of your daily learning through what God's Word has to say on a particular subject.

We will one day reap what we have sown. This is a daunting reality. We need to work hard to intentionally bring our kids up in the fear of the Lord while they are still at home with us. As homeschool parents we are blessed to have conversations that point our children to God's Word for answers, pointing out what the Scripture has to say to them. Never forget the eternal impact this has!

Micah 6:8 reminds us of what we are supposed to be doing, "He has shown you, O man, what is good; And what does the Lord require of you But to do justly, To love mercy, And to walk humbly with Your God?" So from this Scripture, we are to act justly in a world that is unjust. We are to be merciful in a world filled with tough breaks. And we are to walk humbly with God in a world filled with pride and self- sufficiency. We all need to live this out with our children in our classroom. What a gift we have been given to instill Scripture into our dear ones' hearts.

Proverbs 4:23 states, "Keep your heart with all diligence, for out of it spring the issues of life." The study note in my *King James Study Bible* comments that whatever captures the mind captures the man. Take the time to capture teachable moments with your child, time to teach him about the God who loves him more than he can ever imagine! Spend time with your child helping him to be captured by God's love and His Word. Daily read Scripture with your children, pray with them, and talk to them of Jesus as He relates to all aspects of their lives. In 1 Chronicles 28:9 King David is giving instructions to his son Solomon about the building of the temple, "As for you, my son Solomon, know the God of your father, and serve Him with a loyal heart and with a willing mind; for the Lord searches all hearts and understands all the intent of the thoughts. If you seek Him, He will be found by you; but if you forsake Him, He will cast you off forever." Later in the same chapter in verse twenty we read as David speaks to his son Solomon, "Be strong and of good courage, and do it; do not fear nor be dismayed, for the Lord God- my God- will be with you. He will not leave you nor forsake you, until you have finished all the work for the service of the house of the Lord." We do well to speak of these same things to our children, teaching them to seek the Lord with all their hearts, helping them to realize that God will never leave them nor forsake them. We need to teach them to be strong and courageous because they are never alone; God is always with them. We need to model these truths to them and this, dear homeschool parent, is the manifestation of a godly influence in your classroom.

Psalm 128 has been called "the Builder's Psalm". The Psalm tells us,

> "Blessed is everyone who fears the Lord, Who
> walks in His ways.

When you eat the labor of your hands,
You shall be happy, and it shall be well with you.
Your wife shall be like a fruitful vine
In the very heart of your house,
Your children like olive plants
All around your table.
Behold, thus shall the man be blessed
Who fears the Lord.
The Lord bless you out of Zion,
And may you see the good of Jerusalem
All the days of your life.
Yes, may you see your children's children."

The Israelites saw the home as an opportunity to pursue the holy task of "building" sons and daughters. We too should want to follow God's instructions to "build" our children. We lay the foundation of faith. We need to be intentional in our planning of how to teach a child to honor God's Word. Spending time in the classroom with our students affords us the time to do this. All of this intentional building takes much time and effort, so I am thankful for the time spent with them each day.

I spent hours reading Bible stories to our children when they were younger. I subscribe to Christian magazines and we have a closet full of wholesome games. We have many conversations about faith. Church is a weekly priority. And most important of all, David and I try to live out our faith daily in front of their eyes. Children are watching to see if all that we say about Jesus and our faith is real. Just as it takes a lot of time and skill to effectively build a house of brick and wood, it takes a lot of time and skill to build a family home well. Build your children up to have a strong foundation in the knowledge of Jesus Christ, who He is, what He has done, and what He is doing. Remember that a child who is "well built" in the Lord's Ways will have a strong foundation, becoming a builder for the next generation.

We need to fill the role as our children's biggest influencers. There are many belief systems vying for our children's attention. Belief systems opposing Christianity are coming at today's kids with lightning speed from media, friends, cell phones, music, etc. My daughters follow influencers on social media, and just as their name implies, they are hugely influential. Media carries both assumptions and ideas, which are either obvious or subtle, about faith and a Christian worldview. We need to guide our children toward God. Be aware and involved in who and what influences them. Make sure you are the biggest influencer in their lives, influencing them to know God.

Measuring Success

A worldly emphasis is extremely popular today. The world lures the young and the old alike. We are tempted to look out for only ourselves and to gain all that the world has to offer, success seemingly measured by how much a person attains. This attitude is in direct contradiction to God's Word. Truly, we are to seek first the Kingdom of God. Matthew 6:33 spurs us on, "But seek first the kingdom of God, and His righteousness, and all these things shall be added to you."

It is a definite positive in the homeschool world that we know our kids so well, knowing what makes them tick. We have a true heart's desire for them to seek the Lord. We also desire for our children to find a meaningful career. I have homeschool friends whose child has gone to college and others whose child has learned a trade. I know young people who are entrepreneurs and those who are enjoying a job not requiring any post high school education.

Most of us probably agree we want our child to faithfully serve our Lord and Savior. Of course we do, but we can fall into the trap of wanting them to be important in the world's eyes as well. I admit I fight against these thoughts. Upon graduation from college our oldest daughter was hired by a local news station as a reporter, a cutthroat world in many ways. It was a real struggle to not get caught up in the trappings of all of that notoriety. She was a well- known personality and was easily recognized as she went out and about in her television viewing area. She was extremely good at what she did and struggled with whether she should go on to a bigger market, such as D.C. or New York. The move would have been an example of worldly success. After spending four years seeing what goes on behind the scenes, she chose to take a different path. It was a tough decision as the lure of the popularity and the big salary is real, but in the end she chose a life that is better for her family. We can be drawn to what the world teaches is important: money, status, prestige, and power. We can easily want those things for our children. This is human nature. In Romans 12:2 we read, "And be not conformed to this world: but be transformed by the renewing of your mind, that you may prove what is that good, and acceptable, and perfect, will of God." Also Mark 8:36 states, "For what shall it profit a man if he gains the whole world, and loses his own soul?" In the schooling of our children this focus on worldliness can be fought against with God's Word and a Kingdom focus. We can strive, alongside our child, to keep our focus on what is truly significant, which is seeking and knowing God, and living for Him.

Stormie Omartian in her book *The Power of a Praying Wife* says she has observed people who have had actively praying parents seem to find their life's work early. She writes, "While many parents have an agenda for their children, not enough of them seek out God's plan for their lives."[5] We need to be careful that we are not making plans for our children based on what the world tells us. I have had many dreams and plans for my chil-

5. Excerpted from: *The Power of a Praying® Wife,* copyright © 2014 by Stormie Omartian. Published by Harvest House Publishers, Eugene, Oregon 97408. www.harvesthousepublishers.com

dren. I learned through trial and error that God's ways are perfect and mine are perfectly puny. I tell my girls often that God took my well-intentioned plans and miraculously, despite all of my inadequacies, grew them into lovely God-fearing young ladies. I acknowledge and praise Him for that. I could have never dreamed all they have done and are doing. "Great is Thy faithfulness, Lord unto me."

CHAPTER 6

The Beauty of Time

I am blessed by the time I have spent with all of the girls. I can never get the past back, so I am thankful that I choose to invest so much of it in my children. We had many daily rituals that would not have been possible had they been gone from home most of the day at a public or private school.

When our youngest daughter was a toddler we would walk around the house and look at the flowers. We would daily see growth, blooms, hummingbirds, bees, and butterflies. This was an example of a classroom in nature. As we walked, we talked about God's beauty and God's goodness. Through the years, as she grew we discussed important issues such as... why God had to make bees and why hummingbirds are so soft. We have spent countless hours admiring God's handiwork. I know what a blessing I would have missed without that almost daily ritual. It went on for years and a lot was learned in that classroom. I will always cherish the memory of those times and always remember the sweet sound of, "Mom, can we go see what the flowers and bugs are doing today?"

Do *you* have special, daily rituals with your child? What lasting memories are you making? I want to encourage you to start some rituals and traditions. It takes effort and planning, but oh, the memories are worth it. This idea of rituals with your child revisits the idea of intentionality. The opportunity to be intentional in how you spend each day with your child is one of the beauties of homeschool.

I once visited with someone who told me wonderful stories of her rituals with her sons, who are now all three adults with families of their own. When they were little boys in their pajamas ready for bed, this mom would sometimes surprise them by loading them into the car and taking them through the McDonalds drive thru for their favorite treat of French fries. Of course the boys loved this surprise! I was delighted to hear her story, because so many people are in a rat race where life affords no time for such fun and memorable rituals. We as homeschool families have this flexibility of schedule.... we do not have to worry that we are staying up too late for the next school day. I loved this idea so much that when we arrived back home from visiting this family we all piled in the car in our pajamas and made a late night drive thru run to our neighborhood Dairy Queen. (We would rather have ice cream than French fries.) Another ritual we enjoy as a family is our movie night. We have enjoyed many of these through the years, and it is freeing that they do not have to only be a weekend activity. Our kids have fun memories of various weeknights watching favorite movies late into the night, with the benefit of sleeping in the next day. On one such night we watched the movie, "Saving Sarah Cain". It is a movie based on the Beverly Lewis book, *The Redemption of Sarah Cain*.[6] My favorite part of the movie is when the eldest daughter is sharing memories of her mother who has recently passed away. She shares how her mom was intentional in spending time with her and her siblings. She lovingly tells of how her mom took the time to really know her children and participate alongside them in favorite activities. For example, one of the siblings enjoyed walks in the cornfield so the mom

6. Lewis, Beverly, The Redemption of Sarah Cain. Minnesota: Bethany House, 2000.

joined along. Another sibling loved horses so the mom brushed horses with her. The list goes on with each of the remaining siblings. The point is the mom took the time to get to know each of her children individually and to be involved with what was important to them. As a parent who has the gift of time in homeschooling make sure you take advantage of having the time to find out what makes your child "tick". I want my girls to remember our time spent together and think, "Wow, mom knows me so well." It takes being intentional to find out your children's interests, giving them the time and the opportunities to foster their interests. It takes love, time, and insight to know what makes them who they are. Ask God to open your eyes and your heart to them.

I find myself looking back over our homeschool years more often these days as my journey is soon coming to an end. I have climbed the mountain, and I can almost peer at the top. What a view it will be! After seventeen years, I am about to embark on my last homeschool year. Years have flown away. I once wrote in my prayer journal, "Where have the years gone? I know the answer to the question. They have gone past me in the midst of diaper changes, bike rides, tears falling, laughter resonating, jokes told, music played, fights fought, cookies baked, movies watched, words spoken, and through it all love glorious love." As I look at our oldest daughter, who now has a child of her own, I sentimentally remember her in a yellow princess gown, glittery heels on her tiny feet and a straw bonnet perched atop her blonde head of hair. The time that has passed from dress up princess to adulthood has seemingly been "in the blink of an eye". I praise God I have many happy memories tucked away, that our family has had the gift of TIME.

One of my greatest joys as a mom of adult daughters is I can now sit back and watch as they invest their lives in meaning-ful endeavors. I have a front row seat reaping blessings from what God helped me to sow. I watch as our daughter invests in and builds up her son. I remember one particular evening she texted and told me how much our grandson loved to hear her read the "Songs", (his word for Psalms). I was filled with joy to hear she was reading to him from God's Word. She is carrying on tradition and building a foundation of faith. She is modeling what her dad and I did with her. I am thankful for all of those years spent together in our homeschool.

Making homemade memories fosters and grows childish wonder. Childish wonder is a beautiful phrase bringing to mind a sense of awe and joy for life. Childish wonder can be easily nurtured in a homeschooling setting, since we allow our kids time to enjoy what they are learning. I consider the following:

- How many science experiments have I conducted with my daughters through the years?
- How many great books have we read and some for a 2nd or 3rd time?
- How many games have we played?
- How many works of art have they created?
- How many delectable dishes have we "whipped up"?
- How many stories and plays did we recreate?
- How many songs did we sing?

We loved watching the Monarch butterfly metamorphosis each fall. We enjoyed taking field trips, learning so many things firsthand. We had the luxury of taking long walks. We had the freedom to have class outside. We marveled at the beauty of creation. It is wonderful to wonder. As homeschooling families we can enjoy the love of learning. Our girls are all three creative, and their creative outlets have been fueled by wonder. They spent their years at home having quiet time, which often fostered this creativity. They loved to bake, sew, quilt, play, paint, recreate, imagine, etc. So much creativity happens for all of us when we have the time, as well as the encouragement, to explore.

I want my kids to follow the wisdom found in Psalm 46:10, "Be still and know that I am God." I want them to have the time for quiet moments as God speaks to them through His Word. The world, with all its trappings, can be so loud.

I have always been a stay at home mom. I am a firm believer that as moms we need to give to our children as much of our time and attention as we can afford. No one else can love your child the way you can. No matter what the world tries to tell us, a mother is the best person to take care of her own child. No one will do it any better. One of the best parts of being in homeschool is that you get to watch your child's interactions; you have a front row seat to each day in the life of your child. It is pretty cool!

I want you to realize if you have the heart's desire to school your child, then God will give you the wisdom and the strength to do it. When you take the time to learn and school with your child it speaks volumes to him of his importance.

Having the gift of togetherness in your homeschool class-room gives you the opportunity to wake up each day thinking of ways to make your child feel special. I have tried to make an art out of this idea, and I encourage you to do the same. I love to write hand written notes on beautiful stationary, and I write them to my children frequently. We have first and last day of school notes, thank you notes, and just because notes. I create a lot of favorite treats, as I love to cook and bake. I enjoy having beautiful displays of food for my family. My girls love smoothies, and I make them often, pouring them into lovely glasses and topping them with lots of whipped cream! In our family we all love the feeling of clean sheets, so I wash them weekly and have satisfying memories of tucking my girls into crisp, fresh sheets. These ideas may sound simple, but the following quote from American writer Robert Brault reminds us to enjoy them,

"Enjoy the little things for one day you may look back and realize they were the big things." Do not let days and weeks pass
without serving your child and showing him how important he
is. One day these seemingly little things will most likely be re-
membered as the big things. Years ago, I heard Christian author
Anne Ortlund speak at a conference in Richmond, Virginia.
She asked us all to look at everyone as if he or she is wearing a
"make me feel special button". I want to remember this valuable
thought with my own family. Teaching my kids in our homeschool classroom gives me many opportunities to show them
how special they are to me. The beauty of time with them affords us these opportunities.

Jonathan Falwell, pastor at Thomas Road Baptist Church in
Lynchburg, Virginia, writes in his book, *innovatechurch* about
several non- negotiable commitments in his life. His third non-
negotiable commitment on his list asserts: "I will not minister
to my church at the expense of my family."[7] I appreciate the value he places upon his family. I too do not want to do anything
at the expense of my family. I want to have the proper perspective of God first, family second, and ministry third. We try
as a family to keep a somewhat empty slate to schedule these
accordingly.

There are certain activities in our family for which we will
always find the time. We eliminate some things, but make time
for others. We all tend to make time for what is truly important to us. Given the choice, I will always make time for my
family. Case in point, my husband and I attended every one of
our grandson's football games this past fall. It was his first year
playing on the team. He is eight years old. We were intentional
in this attendance, wanting to show him he is important to his
grandma and granddaddy.

We plan to be intentional and involved in many areas of his
life. It takes both planning and saving those Saturday mornings

---

7. Falwell, Jonathan, innovatechurch. Tennessee: B&H Books, 2008.

for football watching. Through the years we have done the same with each of our girls. We have spent myriad hours watching plays, symphonies, ballets, piano recitals, etc. As home educators, we make time for what is truly important, our families.

Being in the midst of COVID 19 this past spring and summer has been challenging for everyone. It saddens me when I hear parents complaining about having their children at home. They complain about having to spend time with them. They can be heard saying, "I cannot wait until summer break is over.", "Why is the Christmas vacation so long?", and "They don't need a fall break." I wonder how the children feel when they hear such comments from their own parents. We need to focus on the positives of being together. We are able to celebrate the firsts and the lasts as the years fly by, savoring these moments in time. We all know they will not come around again. My girls and I have had great, as well as some not so great moments, yet in the midst of it all we have lived life together. My oldest daughter gave me a beautifully framed print with the sentiment, "Together is my favorite place to be." I love it! She knows me so well. Honestly, it is my personality to be totally wrapped up in my family and to celebrate them. I think it is partly the writer in me, the reflective soul; I have journaled about our life: our experiences, interactions, failures, and successes. Reading back through these encounters makes me painfully aware of how quickly time passes.

The walks and talks we have with our children make and shape them. These walks and talks come in the midst of our years of homeschooling. They are spelled TIME.

How can we impart spiritual wisdom to our children if we are not talking and sharing with them about God and Jesus throughout our day? Deuteronomy 6:7 spurs us on to impart spiritual wisdom to our children when we rise up, sit, walk, and lie down. This is daily routine. I will reiterate one of my favorite words, intentional… be **intentional** with your time in spending it well with your family.

Take the time to enjoy your life, making it meaningful. Continual awareness with Jesus keeps us in His perfect peace and helps us to realize what is important as well as what is not, helping us to fill our days with what is truly significant. It allows us to spend our time teaching our children, something truly significant in the scheme of life.

CHAPTER 7

Hurry

I once heard it said that hurry is of the devil. Judging by the way I react when hurried, I tend to agree. I become scatter-brained, easily aggravated and often frustrated when I feel rushed. If I have too much planned and no way of accomplishing anywhere near all of it, I become stressed. Hurry can result in my saying and doing things I regret. William Wilberforce, a British politician, philanthropist, and leader in the movement to abolish the slave trade in the late 1700's, also understood the problem with hurry when he said, "This perpetual hurry of business and company ruins me in soul if not in body." It took me a while in my younger days to learn the lesson of living at a slower pace, realizing that what needs to be accomplished will be, if I rest in the Lord, depending upon Him. He has shown me, through experiences, the importance of prioritizing. As a result, I am no longer a slave to hurry.

Amy Boucher Pye in her ponderings written down in the devotional *Our Daily Bread* asks a thought provoking question for all of us, "Where are you spinning your wheels, wasting time and energy? Ruthlessly eliminate hurry."[8] Ruthlessly, which means without pity or compassion for others, is an intense

---

8. Taken from Our Daily Bread, 2018 by Our Daily Bread Ministries, Grand Rapids, MI. Reprinted by permission. All rights reserved.

word choice. We need to ruthlessly, without pity or compassion, eliminate hurry. We moms and homeschoolers need to not let busyness become a tyrant that controls us, especially when the world tries to tell us that the busier we are, the more valuable we are. We bless our children and others around us when we do not let busyness and hurry control us, when we realize that doing more is not necessarily doing the best.

Our family is rarely in a hurry. I have planned and prioritized to make this so. Since our daughters were young we have had, for the most part, the luxury of an unhurried life. The girls grew up with the feeling they had all the time in the world! There are many positives in living such a life: sharing with each other, enjoying each moment, listening well, and living healthy. The only negative is when we have to be in a hurry, and in life we are inevitably so once in a while, we are in trouble! Something usually gets broken, spilled, forgotten, or messed up.

What about your daily life? Is it too busy? Do you find yourself thinking if only I could spend more time in Bible study and prayer? If only I could slow down and enjoy the daily interactions with my child? If only I could have more time to help others? If only my husband and I could spend more time together? And the list goes on and on for each one of us. C.S. Lewis interestingly points out that no one was busier than Christ, "Our model is the Jesus... of the workshop, the roads, the crowds, the clamorous demands and surly oppositions, the lack of all peace and privacy, the interruptions. For this... is the Divine life operating under human conditions."[9] We need this Divine help in our life as we operate under human conditions. We can ask for His help and learn to live in a way that is less likely to encounter hurry.

We read in Mark 1:32-34 about Jesus in Capernaum, "At evening, when the sun had set they brought to Him all who were

---

9. The Four Loves by CS Lewis copyright CS Lewis Pte Ltd 1960. Used with permission.

sick and those who were demon-possessed. And the whole city was gathered together at the door. Then He healed many who were sick with various diseases, and cast out many demons; and He did not allow the demons to speak, because they knew Him." Jesus was extremely busy, but we find in the next verse (35), that the following day He sought out a solitary place, "Now in the morning, having risen a long while before daylight, He went out and departed to a solitary place: and there He prayed." Jesus made sure He had the time to pray, refresh, and receive direction from His Father. Is your schedule too demanding to seek a solitary place where you can pray and talk with Jesus, where you can hear yourself think? Many people are involved in some kind of sport, activity, or meeting almost every day of the week. You may be running all over town and beyond, trying to get it all done. The result can be a life teetering on exhaustion. I encourage you to eliminate some activities if the adjective frazzled describes you. Follow Jesus's example of carving out quiet time. For me, this means I have to wake each morning at least one hour earlier than the children in my household. Beginning my day in a peaceful, quiet, unhurried way keeps me centered throughout the day. I would go as far to say that I **have** to have this alone time to read Scripture and to pray each morning. Psalm 42:1 speaks of this, "As the deer pants for the water brooks, So pants my soul for You, O God." I need the daily anchor of time spent with my Lord and Savior Jesus Christ. Find a cozy and quiet place, have a cup of coffee or tea, and soak up God's Word and what He has to say to you. It is like climbing into your Father's lap, with your favorite blanket to cuddle up for some hugs and love.

In eliminating too much busyness sometimes we have to eliminate enjoyable and good things when we do not have the time for them. We need to realize it is O.K. to not be involved in everything asked of us. I have been asked to be on many committees and to take part in various activities through the years.

My answer was sometimes "no". I was a pastor's wife for fifteen of our thirty two years of marriage and saying "no" was something I had to learn to do. It is not always favorable for the pastor's wife to say no, just as it is not favorable in some of your current situations. When people ask you to do something, regardless of the situation, they usually want an affirmative answer. Practice saying "no" in the mirror, use this new skill, and do not berate yourself once you have said it! Put your family first. Remember that Satan can sometimes use good things to hinder what is truly best. He wants to keep us just busy enough that we lose track of what is truly important. Take an inventory of your activities, and if you are stretched too thin, eliminate!

It is helpful to be as organized as possible. We all need to organize in a way that best fits our personality and life style. I am a person who cannot let laundry pile up, with the result being that I have to wash it all on Saturday. The thought of piles high of laundry is overwhelming to me. My response is to shut down and do none of it. It is best for me to wash a daily load, since I like to do my chores in small chunks. I enjoy planning meals and cooking them. This is not a chore for me, but if it is for you, there are many great alternatives today. You can sign up with companies that will send you email meal ideas and recipes. There are meal delivery companies delivering healthy and delicious ingredients to your front door just in time to make dinner. Many grocery stores offer online ordering and curbside pick- up. I had none of this when the girls were younger, but I think it would have been helpful. I like to have designated nights for different foods, tacos on Tuesday, make you own pizzas on Friday, grilling out on Saturday, breakfast for dinner on Sunday, etc. It is easier to plan the weekly meals when you only have to vary a few meals a week. Look for ideas in Christian lifestyle books, blog sites, Pinterest, etc. Then make your list of ways to be organized. Enlist your kids to help in keeping your household running smoothly. My girls help with folding the laundry and drying the dishes. They unload the dishwasher most of the time. Now that they are older, we all pitch in to do what needs to be done. When they were younger, they each had specific jobs. Dusting was a favorite when they were little, and I loved that because I hate to dust! I know parents who think it is valuable for their teens to do their own laundry and clean their own bathrooms. A reason given often for this is they will be prepared for college or for the future in living on their own. There is nothing wrong with this thought, but I have personally never felt this way. I want some help, but it is my responsibility to clean our home. My girls went to college and did just fine washing their clothes for the first time and cleaning their dorm bathrooms. Let's be honest, it is not that hard.

I have had more than one mother say to me, "My house is a mess because I spend my time playing with my kids instead of cleaning." Since I have always had a relatively neat home, I do not know how to take this comment. I have probably spent more time with crayons, play dough, dolls, tea parties, and cookie baking than most people, yet I also work hard enough and am organized enough to get the rest accomplished. I have never bought into the idea that I could only do one or the other... why not accomplish both? Actually for me to enjoy doing the fun activities with my children I have to sense some order in my home. I know my husband and daughters appreciate this order as well.

Here are some tips to help you have a tidy home:

- Always put away what you have brought out.
- Limit food, drink, markers, paint, etc. to the kitchen/ kitchen table.
- Set up a weekly cleaning routine (for example, bathrooms cleaned on Monday, floors mopped on Tuesday, sheets washed on Friday).

- Choose certain jobs to be done daily (for me, laundry goes in the wash every morning as soon as I wake up).
- Keep up with dishes (no piles from yesterday).
- Have baskets and shelving for easy storage (there were many days when the kids were little that I would go around the house, scooping up all the toys and books into baskets, just before my husband arrived home from work).
- Make the beds every morning.

Here are some organizational helps:

- Make a weekly grocery list
- Grocery shop only once or twice a week
- Plan all of your meals for the week (it helps me to have designated evenings for designated meals such as Taco Tuesday and Homemade Pizza night every Friday)
- Use a crock pot often
- Be a list person
- Have a family calendar with all activities listed on it
- Set a timer for certain tasks

Gustavo Razzetti in his article written for *PsychologyToday. com* states, "The secret of being more productive lies in choosing what to do- and doing it right- instead of doing more and more. When you are busy, you don't have time to think, reflect or enjoy. You are running from one task to another without being present. Your mind needs space. Silence helps us reflect. Serendipity attracts new ideas. Distance brings perspective."[10]

Seleni.org gives this advice:

- Start small

---

10. Gustavo Razzetti, author and CEO at Fearless Culture (www.fearless-culture.design).

- Set parameters around your workday
- Let some things go
- Realize that slowing down is important
- Schedule down time

You can take these ideas and make them your own, using them to enhance your family's schedule. Work hard even when the going gets tough. There is no room for perpetual laziness.

There are many Proverbs that speak of laziness. Here are two:

- Proverbs 15:19 has this to say, "The way of the lazy man is like a hedge of thorns, But the way of the upright is a highway."
- In Proverbs chapter 21, verse 25 we read, "The desire of the lazy man kills him, for his hands refuse to labor."

We are warned in God's Word to not be lazy, so if this is a problem for you, ask God for help to become a hard worker. We have a serious job to do, a blessed job, and we need to be diligent in fighting against the sin of laziness.

With all of this said, I realize how difficult keeping a house in order can be. It is easy to talk about a neat home but the reality of the day is that sometimes everything ends up being a mess. People have the idea that since we are home all day we can more easily accomplish all household tasks. This is not the reality; we are busy teaching our children. The day is full, between schooling your child in all subjects and taking him to all of his activities, you are one busy person! But for the norm, our school room and home should have a sense of order to be productive. In the midst of the activities of the day I like to reflect on my favorite Scriptures and my relationship with the Lord. I never want to take these for granted. I want to live each day well!

Striving for a Balanced Life

I want to be balanced. I want to have daily time for worship, work, rest and play. I want to have my Bible read, prayers lifted up, school lessons accomplished, meals planned, household organized, exercise time, and for me personally, a time for hot tea! All of these areas accomplished because of His mercy, grace, joy, strength, and wisdom. All of these accomplished in the midst of our homeschooling day. With deliberate planning and intentionality, it is possible! Eliminating television, computer time, and time spent on a cellphone can free up a lot of extra time.

Dr. James Dobson in his book *What Wives Wish Their Husbands Knew About Women* writes the following, "Prescription for a Happier and Healthier Life: Resolve to slow your pace: learn to say no gracefully; resist the temptation to chase after more pleasures, hobbies, and more social entanglements; Then 'hold the line' with the tenacity of a tackle for a professional football team."[11] I love this reminder and the seriousness it conveys.

---

11. Some content taken from *What Wives Wish Their Husbands Knew About Women* by Dr. James Dobson. Copyright 1975. Used by permission of Tyndale House Publishers, a Division of Tyndale House Ministries. All rights reserved.

CHAPTER 8

A Homeschool Senior's Perspective

Hi Y'all! I'm the youngest daughter of the author, Steffanie. I'm here to tell you a little about my journey as a homeschooler. Hopefully this will give you a peek into the life of a homeschool student.

As a teenager I have found that almost every conversation I have with my peers eventually leads to the question: where do you go to school? As I brace myself for the deluge of questions that will come with my answer, I smile and tell them I am homeschooled. I have gotten a variety of responses anywhere from "I wish I was homeschooled!" to "What do you do all day?" I have even gotten a few "You don't act homeschooled!"! I'm never really sure how to take that one! But with every response there is a common denominator: **misconceptions**. Many times the people who say they wish they were homeschooled go on to comment about how nice it would be to wear their pajamas all day and do school in bed. I then tell them that I get up and get ready every day and do school work at the kitchen table. The people who ask what I do all day often assume that I spend my day doing very little studying and then spend the rest of my time staring at a wall wishing I had things to do. I then go on to explain how busy I actually am and how even though I am at home, I still have a routine that I follow. The people who are surprised by my outgoing personality have preconceived notions that homeschoolers are socially awkward and unable to hold conversations. Yes, I am able to interact and participate in social situations (shocked gasps)! I have always been an over achiever, so these misconceptions and assumptions about my work ethic and school day have always bothered me. I used to feel the need to explain every detail about my life and school day to validate my lifestyle. But as I grew older I realized that I do not need to explain! Even after I explained every detail of my school day, people were still skeptical. Both of my sisters are successful women in their careers, and I am working hard to be successful as well! The results speak for themselves. I keep myself focused on doing my best, and I remember what 1 Corinthians 10:31 says: to do EVERYTHING for the glory of God.

As I previously mentioned I am one busy gal! I am a senior in high school who juggles school, extracurricular activities, and family and friend time! I am a violinist who plans on pursuing music as a career. This means lots of practice time! Homeschooling gives me lots of flexibility to get everything done. I wake up anywhere from 7:30 am to 8:30 am, depending on how tired I am or how much work I have to do that day. Being sleepy during the day does not help productivity! I typically do all of my school work in the morning. This does not mean that I do less work than a public school student. I simply am able to work more quickly and use my time more efficiently than if I were in a classroom. I have been homeschooled my entire life, except for a semester in second grade when I attended a small private Christian school. My parents wanted me to have the experience, as well the option to have a different school setting. Every day I finished my work before some of the other students. I would then read the books on the bookshelves in our classroom. By the end of the semester, I had read every book in the classroom! Needless to say the experience I received in a non-homeschool setting was not one I enjoyed! I finished my second grade year at home and have never looked back! Without the hindrance of a classroom setting, I am able to work quickly and efficiently. I work on school assignments all morning, have lunch, and then I get to practicing! Violin practice takes up most of the afternoon. Sometimes I have other things to do in the afternoon, so I have to fit practicing into the evening. I have weekly violin lessons, orchestra practice, and church youth group. Time has a way of disappearing! Homeschooling gives me and my family the reins on our schedule. I have friends who attend public and private schools who are always talking about how stressed they are. By the end of the school year they are exhausted and burnt out. They tell me about some of the silly and useless things they have to do in school. These are the moments that I am particularly thankful for the blessing of homeschooling! Being in charge of my own routine is truly a blessing!

Being homeschooled has provided me with unique opportunities and time to explore my interests. Many times we have taken advantage of our flexible schedule and done things that would not have been possible if I had not been homeschooled. As before mentioned, I am a violinist and I currently take lessons two hours away from my home town. This is a prime example of homeschooling opening up my schedule because I make the trip on a weekday. Many of the wonderful and happy memories that I have would not have been made if I had not been homeschooled.

I truly believe if I had not been homeschooled I would not be as close to my family as I am. Being homeschooled provides PLENTY of family time! When your parents are the teachers and your siblings are your classmates you get to know them pretty well! My parents and I have always been close, and we love spending time together. Spending the greater part of everyday with them is something I enjoy. Being homeschooled has made our family tight-knit, and the time I have been blessed to have with them is something I will cherish forever!

As far as being "socialized" goes, I think I have had plenty "socialization"! I have always attended homeschool co-ops and have met interesting and diverse people. One of the things I love about my fellow homeschoolers is their ability to embrace their uniqueness! We can have fun and just be ourselves together! Every year we have a "Heritage Ball", which is a fun dance where we all dress up and participate in Colonial style dances. It is my favorite event of the season, and we all have a ball (no pun intended!). Spinning and dosie-doing to "Yankee Doodle" may not be everyone's cup of tea (don't knock it 'till you've tried it!), but it is yet another example of the unique social environment a homeschool community creates. There are girls attending who have sewn their own colonial style dresses while others are wearing this year's latest fashion trends, but we all support each other and have fun in the process. I have found that many times public school students are exclusive and cold. They do not go out of their way to be welcoming. I have found that being homeschooled has pushed me to be MORE social than most. I am a social and friendly person who loves to meet new people, so in large groups I often have to initiate the conversation and make new friendships. I have learned to make friends with anyone and everyone! Having the experience of being the "outsider" has given me a fresh perspective and compassion for the more quiet or excluded people in the group. I hate seeing people left out, and try my hardest to keep everyone together and in the group. Being homeschooled has shaped my personality, helping me to be the friendly person I am today. It has also given me a whole lot of experience conversing with adults. You spend a lot of time with your parents and learn how to communicate well. My parents have taught me how to be a professional young woman, which is a skill I would not have learned in any public school classroom. I have not missed out one bit when it comes to friendships and time with others, but instead I have built friendships and have learned a lot about how to be a good friend and a good communicator.

Being at home teaches you creative ways to occupy your time. In the recent Coronavirus pandemic I have been spending more time at home than usual. I still have plenty to do! Being homeschooled has given me the experience to know how to best fill my time. I have practiced, read, spent time outside, tried new workouts, baked, and even made an inspiration/vision wall during quarantine! Homeschooling has given me time in the past to discover my likes and interests, so I have easily been able to fill my time. Homeschooling makes one content and at peace with being at home. I love my time spent at home, and even sometimes opt out of social events just to spend more time there! I believe that homeschooling has given me this contentment and creativity to be able to avoid boredom. I once heard a quote that said, "Smart girls don't get bored." I LOVE this quote! Homeschooling has fostered my love of learning and creativity. I love broadening my horizons, whether this means going out on a road trip or curling up with a good book.

Homeschooling has given me a good work ethic. In the book *Little Women* by Louisa May Alcott, the girl's mother or "Marmee" lets them have a week off from chores and school. Marmee does this as a lesson to the girls, knowing they will soon come to appreciate the work. At first the girls are absolutely thrilled and spend their time lazing around. Eventually this lazy lifestyle gets old, and they are eager to get back to work. This is one of my all-time favorite books EVER, and I think that there is much to be learned from this particular fictitious family, but this instance gives a good insight into a day of homeschooling. I have homeschooled friends who do not work hard and do not spend their time efficiently. They often tell me they wish they could do as much as I do, and say they are always bored. They have not learned to appreciate hard work! Marmee knew that working hard was important and taught her children this important lesson. I have been blessed to have parents like Marmee, who have taught me the value of hard work. When you homeschool you have the option to slack off, to put off until tomorrow, etc., but working hard pays off! My family has instilled a good work ethic in me that has served me well through grade school and has prepared me for college and beyond.

One of the greatest and most important things about homeschool is that it helps strengthen your relationship with the Lord. I spend lots of time with my parents, observing their Godly example daily. They always impart wisdom that brings me closer to God. I study Christian curriculum that helps me understand the world around me through a Jesus-tinted lens. I am often surrounded by like-minded teens who share my love for the Lord. In our daily homeschool agenda reading the Bible is a central focus, and prayer is a big part of our day. I thank God that I have the opportunity to learn more about Him every day during school!

So to quickly recap here is a list of some of my favorite things about homeschooling:

- Able to study God's Word as well as learn from a Christian viewpoint
- Spending time with family
- Having a flexible schedule
- Making unique friendships
- Learning to adapt in social situations
- Fostering creativity and a good work ethic

To conclude my chapter in this book, I want you to know that homeschooling has been one of the best parts of my life. I would not have traded it for the world! As I write this I am preparing for my senior year of high school. I cannot believe how fast it has gone! I still remember kindergarten when I had my Dora the Explorer math book and would sing and dance along to the days of the week and months of the year! Time has FLOWN! I am preparing for college but I know I have had years of training to prepare me for whatever comes my way, and I have the years I spent at home with the people I love most to thank for that. Is homeschooling for everyone? No, not necessarily. But as a homeschool student I encourage you to give it a shot! It will be one crazy yet amazing ride! To once again return to *Little Women* I would like to close this chapter with one of my favorite quotes from the book: "Watch and pray, Dear, never get tired of trying, and never think it is impossible to conquer your fault."[12] Blessings to all of you on your homeschool journey!

---

12. Alcott, Louisa May, *Little Women*. Boston, Massachusetts: Roberts Brothers, 1880.

CHAPTER 9

Last Minute Musings

A s I write this final chapter I am feeling a little anxious. Did I tell you enough? Have I helped you enough? Do you now feel equipped to try this homeschooling thing on your own? I so want this book to help you feel empowered and ready to embark on your own homeschool journey. Here is a list of what I wish I would have known when I started all those years ago:

What I Wish I Would Have Known Back at the Beginning:

- Daily Bible reading and prayer time with my children is vital.
- Daily personal time with God reading Scripture and praying is critical.
- My husband is my helper.
- I know what is best for my children.
- A schedule should not be the end all.
- It is O.K. not to be O.K.
- I am not perfect.
- I can send my children to their rooms with their doors closed and not feel guilty.
- I can reach out for help.

- I need an accountability partner.
- I need a day off once in a while.
- My children will be fine if I skip a school lesson, or even a school day.
- Skeptics will always be around.
- Homeschool is the best education method there is.
- God is in control.
- I am not in control.
- Homeschool conventions and Classical Conversations parent practicums are worthwhile and helpful.
- Sometimes it is best to drop it and come back to it later.
- Some days I do not like homeschool.
- A student's attitude changes with the wind.
- Treats and rewards are my friends.
- Homeschool and education magazines give ideas for fun activities.
- I can teach all subjects well.
- God gives us more than we can ever ask or imagine!

As a homeschool mom our kids witness our triumphs and our failures. They truly know us. I tell my girls, "I know I have not done everything well and really messed up sometimes, but you know the real me, the good and the not so good, the pretty and the not so pretty. Through it all you know one definite; I am the mom who tries and will continue to try." I can breathe a sigh of relief, I am doing just fine! You will too!

God Will Enable You

When God calls you to do something, He will enable you to do it. 1 Thessalonians 5:24 states, "He who calls you is faithful, who also will do it." I held on to this Scripture as I began my homeschool journey. I believed it. I still believe it. I have lived it over and over again. Be bold and confident that He who works in you will complete the work just as Philippians 1:6 tells us, "Being confident of this very thing, that He who has begun a good work in you will complete it until the day of Jesus Christ." There have been many days when I have rested in this Scripture and in the knowledge that God knows my heart and knows that it is my heart's desire to raise our girls to follow hard after Him. It is a comfort to know that in all aspects of our schooling, God knows our hearts. Psalm 37:4 gives us a wonderful promise, "Delight yourself also in the Lord; And He shall give you the desires of your heart." We desire to homeschool our children well.

Another promise is found in Colossians 1:29, "I also labor, striving according to His working which works in me mightily." He is working in us in a mighty way when we seek His help and His guidance in the instruction of our children. It is He who works mightily, not us. We need to labor and strive according to what He shows us in the Scriptures, not forgetting that He is the Mighty One in control of it all. Praise Him that He is in control, and be a willing vessel to be used by Him.

I like to reflect on Psalm 90:17 when I think of my homeschool journey, "And let the beauty of the Lord our God be upon us and establish the work of our hands for us, Yes, establish the work of our hands." He establishes the work of our hands when we surrender and allow Him to do so. Our homeschool classroom is a beautiful sight when this happens. Our Teacher walking alongside us, makes all the difference in our classroom. Jennifer Schuldt, contributing writer to *Our Daily Bread*, shares, "Our life with Jesus is more like a duet than a solo performance. It is only by His power that I can play at all."[13] Isn't that a beautiful thought? We are playing a duet with Jesus in the education of our children; never try to go solo.

In Acts Chapter 8 the angel of the Lord speaks to Philip and tells him to go to Gaza. He is obedient and goes to explain the

---

13. Taken from Our Daily Bread, 2020 by Our Daily Bread Ministries, Grand Rapids, MI. Reprinted by permission. All rights reserved.

Scriptures to an Ethiopian eunuch. I have always loved Philip's instant obedience to go. I want to be just as obedient and go where the Lord leads me. Since I know with all certainty that God's will is for me to teach my children to know Him and His ways, I have chosen to homeschool. I am confident that teaching them at home has been Spirit led. I am also confident that God has enabled me and blessed me through it all. Ephesians 3:20 causes me to smile as I reflect upon my life, "Now to Him who is able to do exceedingly abundantly above all that we ask or think, according to the power that works in us, to Him be glory in the church by Christ Jesus to all generations, forever and ever. Amen." Wow, almost two decades of learning at home with my girls! Now that is immeasurably more than I ever asked or imagined! One of my all-time favorite classics is *Peter Pan*. I love the quote, "Would you like an adventure now, or shall we have our tea first?" My girls and I were blessed to be able to do both and to do them often.

The following poem is one I wrote about my homeschool journey and what it has looked like for me:

"Collaborating With Jesus"

You walk before me,
As I wake to begin my day.
You prepare the way in our classroom,
And You are the leader in our home education.
You walk beside me daily,
Giving me love, inspiration, discernment and peace.
You lighten my load when the day drags on and everything feels heavy.
You tell me I am never alone,
Even on those dark days when I feel isolated.

You bring joy into my life through silliness and
laughter with my children.
You give me the support and encouragement I
need at just the right time,
Love from my husband, a kind note, a friend's
text, or a surprising comment from one of the
girls, all showing me I can, and will, keep traveling the road less traveled.
You give me success, as I lead my children to
seek and to follow You.
You raise me up to confidently continue.
Joy, peace, hope, love—
Fruits of collaborating with You.

I am so thankful I had the faith to take the first steps to homeschool. Each member of our family has reaped the benefits. As
Dr. Martin Luther King Jr. insightfully said, "faith is taking the
first steps even when you don't see the whole staircase." We
certainly did not see the whole staircase back at the beginning,
but it is a blessing now to see how many stairs we have climbed
and to now be able to enjoy the view near the top. It is truly
amazing! May you have the faith to take that first step, and all
of the steps thereafter.

I do not claim to have arrived at the destination of perfec-
tion in homeschooling. None of us can claim such. I still, after
all these years, can be too hard on myself. Did I teach them
enough? Do they know enough? Are they prepared enough?
Have I given them enough opportunities and experiences? But
now that I am on the other side, the one near the end, I can
clearly see the multiple benefits and blessings of our chosen
path. I see that I did do enough, more than enough! My daughters were and are prepared for life and a life of abundance. I am
forever grateful for this blessed journey!

There are lessons I continue to learn. One of my newest lessons learned in having adult and nearly adult children is that I love my kids not for what they have done, are doing, or will do, but just for who they are, warts and all. Pretty cool, huh? Just as my Heavenly Father loves me with my warts and all! I praise God for His infinite mercy and grace. I praise Him for our three beautiful children whom I have been able to learn with for so many years.

In Hebrew the word *Hesed* is sometimes translated "steadfast love." Steadfast love is a love that is faithful and reliable; it is a love shown in action, dependability, and in working for the good of the person who is loved. You are the one sharing *Hesed* in the schooling of your child! You can live in a way that shows this love daily! You are valuable! My prayer is that this book has touched you in the way that our Almighty God would have you be touched. I pray that we will all prayerfully, diligently, and whole-heartedly seek His face in all that we do with our children. Let us not grow weary in the task that has been set before us. Proverbs 14:1 tells us, "Every wise woman builds her house." Let us all be wise women who build our houses well. Let us realize how blessed we are to be able to homeschool our kids, building them up for the next generation.

Psalm 90:12 rings true to us homeschoolers, "So teach us to number our days, that we may apply our hearts unto wisdom." Let us count the days and make them truly count each day as we school our children. And let us do all for the glory of God, always remembering it is the Lord Jesus Christ whom we are serving. May God bless your diligent homeschooling, and may He give you a burning desire to do the very best job that you can in His Strength, until the day when you hear the words of Matthew 25:21, "Well done, good and faithful servant." To God be the glory!

About the Author

Steffanie Williams lives in Roanoke, Virginia. She has been married to her husband David for thirty two wonderfully lived years. She is mom to Katie, Emily and Mary Ruth. She is grandma to Noah David. Steffanie was born and raised in Virginia and has lived all over the state she calls home. In her spare time she loves spending time with her family out on the lake, reading a good book, or cooking a great meal. She began writing *Parenting with Passion* back in 2005 when her children were fourteen, eleven, and two. After many years she felt led to take the "bones" of the original text and rewrite it into a home-schooling book. *Eww.... You Homeschool? ~Help for Successful Homeschooling~* is the result. Steffanie reflects, "I am no more an expert on parenting than the next person, but I do know quite a bit about homeschooling after schooling my children at home for the past 18 years." She hopes this book will be both helpful and encouraging to you the reader. She would love to hear from you on her Steffanie Williams – Author Facebook page.